JOURNEY 101

Daily Readings

JOURNEY 101
Steps to the Life God Intends

This three-part basic faith course is designed to teach what it means to know, love, and serve God. Each of the three separate, interactive six-week studies uses a group teaching format, combining video teaching and small group table breakouts. The three studies include:

KNOWING GOD. Explore the good news of the Bible and discover Bible study tools and resources to deepen your understanding of God and the Scriptures.

LOVING GOD. Experience spiritual transformation through spiritual practices that will help you fall more in love with God and grow in your relationship with God and others.

SERVING GOD. Understand the biblical context for service that will enable you to use your hands, your time, and your spiritual gifts to serve others and share Christ.

Components:

Participant Guide (1 for each study)—Six interactive session guides with space for responding to questions and activities and recording personal reflections.

Leader Guide (1 for each study)—Six complete session guides for facilitating a group with additional leader helps.

Daily Readings—Serves as the devotional companion for the entire three-part Journey 101 series. Ninety devotions (thirty devotions per study).

DVD—3-disc set (120 minutes per DVD/study; 360 minutes total)

Preview Book—Provides an overview of the topics covered in the entire three-part Journey 101 course.

Leader Kit—One each of the components listed above.

Carol Cartmill

Jeff Kirby

Michelle Kirby

JOURNEY 101

Daily Readings
by Ben Simpson

Abingdon Press
Nashville

JOURNEY 101
Daily Readings

Copyright © 2013 by Abingdon Press
All rights reserved.

This book is printed on acid-free, elemental chlorine–free paper.

Library of Congress Cataloging-in-Publication applied for.

ISBN 978-1-4267-6645-9

13 14 15 16 17 18 19 20 21 22—10 9 8 7 6 5 4 3 2 1

MANUFACTURED IN THE UNITED STATES OF AMERICA

Contents

Loving God

Contents

Introduction

Journey 101 is a three-course study designed to help guide you on this journey of knowing, loving, and serving God. As you embark on the journey, it is vitally important that you know the destination, the place where you want to end up. And that destination is to become a deeply committed Christian—a person who knows, loves, and serves God with increasing passion and dedication. The courses in this series will help you to answer some important questions:

- How does a deeply committed Christian grow to know God more deeply?

- How would my life be transformed if I loved God with the fullness of my heart?

- How should I, as a deeply committed Christian, be serving in the world?

You will consider these questions in a group setting, using the Journey 101 guidebooks and DVDs. You will also find it helpful to read, ponder, and pray about the questions on your own. I've written this book of daily readings to help you do just that.

How to Use This Book

The book consists of ninety devotions—thirty each on Knowing God, Loving God, and Serving God. Each of these three sections, like the three Journey 101 courses, is designed for use during a six-week period. The weekly devotion topics match the weekly course topics, so the devotions will support and complement what happens each week in the group.

I've written each devotion to include a Scripture reading, an illustration or story, and a brief written prayer. There are five entries per week. I suggest reading one entry per day, Monday through Friday, resting on Saturday, and attending worship on Sunday. Place this book on your nightstand or on the corner of your desk, somewhere you will see it each day. When you have a free moment, quiet your heart and mind, then take up the book and read.

If you fall behind schedule, don't worry. Simply begin again. If you picked up this book of daily readings apart from the Journey 101 course, the meditations may still prove helpful in moving you toward Christian maturity. The practice of Bible reading, thoughtful engagement with the text, and daily prayer has long been a powerful avenue for connecting with God, opening a possibility for life transformation. Whether using this book or another resource, make this practice a habit.

My Hope for You

In the Book of Colossians, Paul writes, "He is the one we proclaim, admonishing and teaching everyone with all wisdom, so that we may present everyone fully mature in Christ. To this end I strenuously contend with all the energy Christ so powerfully works in me" (Colossians 1:28-29). Like Paul, my hope for you is that you would become fully mature in Christ.

For those taking their first steps on the Christian journey, I am excited for you! I want great things for you. I want you to know, love, and serve God with all that you have and all that you are. I want you to "shine . . . like stars in the sky" (Philippians 2:15). Follow Christ, and you will.

For those farther along the Christian journey, I am glad to come alongside as you take your next steps. I pray you will encourage others as Barnabas did, "a good man, full of the Holy Spirit and faith," and that as a result many would come to know Jesus and reach maturity in faith (Acts 11:24).

Finally, know that all who read this book are included in my prayers. Though I might not ever learn your name, God knows all things. I have asked, and will continue to ask, that God will use these simple words to bring many to know, love, and serve God.

May God bless you as you walk along the way.

Ben Simpson

Knowing God

Receiving Christ

1. PURSUING THE HIGHEST GOOD

This is what the LORD says:

"Let not the wise boast of their wisdom
  or the strong boast of their strength
  or the rich boast of their riches,
but let the one who boasts boast about this:
  that they have the understanding to know me,
that I am the LORD, who exercises kindness,
  justice and righteousness on earth,
  for in these I delight,"
    declares the LORD.

Jeremiah 9:23-24

One of the great passions of my life is the game of basketball. I love to play, watch, and study the game. I've spent a great deal of energy obtaining knowledge of the history, technique, and strategy of basketball. And like most who gain mastery over a subject, I like to show off what I know.

Your great love might be something else. As Jeremiah writes, it might be wisdom or strength or wealth. It might be family or career or education. I would bet there is something in your life you have worked hard to attain, and that you'd name as your highest good. You might be said to "boast" in it. It may be a good thing.

But it is not the ultimate thing.

God is the ultimate thing. And we're called to know him.

Think carefully: If there is a God, and God wishes to be in relationship with us, would it not be of highest value to discover and pursue that relationship to its fullest? And if God is the highest good, is it not true that intelligence, physical strength, and wealth pale in comparison to the reward of knowing the one who is the fount of all wisdom, giver of all strength, and provider of all wealth?

Jeremiah also tells us that God "exercises kindness, justice and righteousness on earth." If this were so, would it not be true that God would work toward these purposes in our lives? Perhaps we should get to know this God, so that we might humbly discover how to pursue his ways in all our endeavors.

Seek knowledge of God. Then everything else takes on a new significance.

Lord, you have brought me to a place in my journey where I desire to know you. May I take hold of your great love as you have taken hold of me. May I stake my identity solely upon you and live accordingly. Amen.

2. A NEW IDENTITY

But God chose the foolish things of the world to shame the wise; God chose the weak things of the world to shame the strong. God chose the lowly things of this world and the despised things—and the things that are not—to nullify the things that are, so that no one may boast before him. It is because of him that you are in Christ Jesus, who has become for us wisdom from God—that is, our righteousness, holiness and redemption. Therefore, as it is written: "Let the one who boasts boast in the Lord."

1 Corinthians 1:27-31

My friend Mike is a brilliant man, a good husband and father, and an excellent teacher. He is also a songwriter and musician, and leads worship at his church. He is someone I really admire and respect.

But on more than one occasion when I have lifted up his strengths, Mike has quoted to me these words from 1 Corinthians. Mike does so with a wry smile—he's small of stature—but he also wishes to remind us both that the good I see in his life is rooted in another source. Mike is aware of the power of God, who has changed his life in Christ Jesus. He wishes to give glory to God for every good thing he does.

One of the great discoveries that comes in knowing God is a renewed understanding of the world around you. In Paul's words above, he suggests that in Christ, God has turned everything upside down. The foolish shame the wise. The weak shame the strong. The lowly and "things that are not" are given favor. A great leveling has taken place. It's knowing God that matters, not our merits.

Knowledge of God also brings about a new understanding of our self. Many of our shortcomings, personality flaws, and personal failings are rooted in human sinfulness. Our strengths and talents are, of course, things we have worked diligently to improve and refine, but we can ultimately see them anew as God's gifts. God redeems us from our sinfulness, one expression of which is our own self-righteousness. We've been given a new life.

It is Christ who is our life—his wisdom, righteousness, holiness, and redemption—for we are *in him*. Knowing this changes our outlook.

Christ Jesus, you are my wisdom, righteousness, holiness, and redemption. May I worship and serve you today. Amen.

3. THE SCOPE OF KNOWLEDGE

*Great is the L*ORD *and most worthy of praise;*
  his greatness no one can fathom.
One generation commends your works to another;
  they tell of your mighty acts.
They speak of the glorious splendor of your majesty—
  and I will meditate on your wonderful works.
They tell of the power of your awesome works—
  and I will proclaim your great deeds.
They celebrate your abundant goodness
  and joyfully sing of your righteousness.

Psalm 145:3-7

While human beings cannot know God exhaustively, we can know enough to have confidence in God.

Consider an automobile. Vehicles are designed by engineers. Each design is carefully examined and evaluated by executives, safety officials, and assembly specialists. Each car is then produced, shipped to a dealership, and sold.

Most people who buy a car do not ask for blueprints or extensive readouts from roadway testing. Most do not carefully consider the engine housing, the frame's ability to withstand collisions, or electrical wiring. Most consult popular consumer guides or other roadway safety resources, talk with friends and family, and make a purchase, trusting that the vehicle will be in good working order.

Much of what we believe is accepted on the basis of authority. We don't have to know everything to accept a general truth, only enough to believe that those in authority can be trusted. Oftentimes, trusting is a first step on the path to greater knowledge. For example, before taking an automobile for a test drive, we must trust that the engine will start when we turn the ignition. If it does not, we may lose faith that the car is worth the investment. But if it cranks and handles smoothly, we will grow in confidence and knowledge of the car.

Christians have long confessed that God is great, good, loving, and just—beyond what we can know. But while we cannot know everything, we can know enough to put our faith in God. Like the psalmist, our confidence is built on what God has done in the past, both in the stories of Scripture, and, on occasion, in our own lives. Once we take a step, trusting that God will work for our good as he has worked for the good of others in the past, we grow in knowledge of him.

Lord, please take my faith and give it increase. May my belief grow to a sure knowledge of your grace. Amen.

4. RESCUED FROM SIN

For all have sinned and fall short of the glory of God.

Romans 3:23

The great theologian Reinhold Niebuhr once observed, "The doctrine of original sin is the only empirically verifiable doctrine of the Christian faith."[1] One does not have to look long and hard to find assurance that Niebuhr was right. Turn on the news. Open the newspaper. Look in the mirror.

Some may find this notion disconcerting, that all people have an inclination to sin, deny knowledge of God, and act accordingly. It is more comforting to think of our neighbors and ourselves as flawed or broken rather than sinful. We all make mistakes, we all blunder into hurting others, right? But why are we often convinced that we not only have been wounded, but wronged? Sin is not simply a matter of hurt feelings but of justice, and the ultimate standard for justice is found in God's very being, God's perfect glory.

This has implications for knowing God. We will consider two. First, acknowledging our sinful condition should humble us, not through guilt but greater self-knowledge. People who understand sin as the common plight of human beings can never believe they are better than anyone else. They are humble. Understanding sin leads to a deeper and more complete understanding of how we demonstrate grace.

Second, as Paul noted in 2 Corinthians 7:10, knowing ourselves as sinful should lead us to repentance and cause us to seek healing and restoration. This healing cannot come from within but must come from God. In Romans 3:24, Paul writes that "all are justified freely by his grace through the redemption that came by Christ Jesus." Despite the fact we are sinners, Christ died to reconcile all people to God (Romans 5:8). As foretold so powerfully in Isaiah 53:5, "By his wounds we are healed."

The gospel is simply this: You are loved more than you ever have dared hope. God's work on the cross in the person of Jesus Christ is the assurance and confirmation of that love. Christ laid down his life to redeem you from sin, restore you to health, and guide you to fullness of life.

You can know God's powerful love. Once you encounter it, you will be changed. Grace, not sin, has the last word. Rejoice.

Father, help me to live by your grace, to repent of my sin, and to look to you for a new heart, a new life. Amen.

5. A NEW UNDERSTANDING

" 'My son,' the father said, 'you are always with me, and everything I have is yours. But we had to celebrate and be glad, because this brother of yours was dead and is alive again; he was lost and is found.'"

Luke 15:31-32

The parable of the prodigal son, also known as the parable of the two sons, is one of Jesus' most beloved teachings. In it, a son leaves home, squanders his inheritance, hits rock bottom, and returns home to a loving embrace from his father. A second son, who obeys his father carefully, also distances himself from his parent, only to be beckoned back to fellowship. Start to finish, this parable is a compelling tale. We can easily place ourselves in the story. If you are not familiar with the story, read it. As you read, think carefully about what Jesus communicates about God's grace.

In Luke 15, Jesus was surrounded by "sinners and tax collectors." This fact caused the religious leaders around Jesus to grumble and say, "Look who this man associates with." Jesus then tells three stories, inviting the riffraff to see God's love for them and challenging the righteous to reconsider their understanding of God.

Why did Jesus teach in parables? Oftentimes, Jesus' parables help us discover a new understanding of God and God's action in the world. These stories can leave us exposed, challenging some of our notions of God. They can also fill a gap, bringing us into an encounter with God in which we come to know him better.

How do you understand God? Where does your understanding align with sound teaching that is grounded in Scripture and the Christian tradition? Which of your beliefs are well developed and strong?

Where might you have a false view of God? Disciples who are wise will be open to correction. It may be that some of your assumptions about God are not well reasoned or simply false.

As you embark on this study, it might be worthwhile to think through your beliefs about God. Write them down on a piece of paper. What is God like? Whom does God love? What kind of life does God call us to live?

Now ask Jesus to teach you throughout this study. Receive him, and be open to his direction.

Jesus, your teachings are profound and challenging. May I remain open to instruction, so that I can experience you as you truly are. Amen.

Comprehending Christ's Teachings

6. ENCOUNTERING THE CHRIST

Again Jesus began to teach by the lake. The crowd that gathered around him was so large that he got into a boat and sat in it out on the lake, while all the people were along the shore at the water's edge. He taught them many things by parables, and in his teaching said: "Listen! A farmer went out to sow his seed."

Mark 4:1-3

I live in the state of Kansas, where Jayhawk basketball is incredibly popular. Graduates of the university are passionate about their team. The coaches and players are constantly being evaluated against the greats of the past, and on game day Allen Fieldhouse is sold out. I've been at games where the decibel reading has exceeded 120, comparable to the sound of a sandblaster or a loud rock show; 125 decibels is where pain begins.

Jesus created a similar stir in his time. When he visited a community, it would have been like a politician arriving to deliver a stump speech, or a once-in-a-lifetime performance by a musical virtuoso. Often, when we think of Jesus we picture him picking dandelions or quietly contemplating peace. We do not think of an unparalleled intellect preaching a revolutionary message, accompanied by signs and wonders. Healings were reported. Demons were cast out. Outcasts were being restored, the dead raised, and those thought "unclean" were welcomed. Controversy followed Jesus because of what he was saying and doing.

Can we take Jesus this seriously today? He leaves us little choice, if we truly understand who he is. C. S. Lewis famously argued that we cannot consider Jesus only a good man or a great teacher—either he is a liar or lunatic, or he is Lord.[2] If our reaction to Jesus is tepid, we have not yet beheld him. But if we experience either strong rejection or profound attraction, we are beginning to see.

In Mark 4, we read that people eagerly waited to hear what Jesus had to say, and we can imagine that they matched or exceeded the fervor of the most passionate Kansas basketball fan. Do you pay Jesus that much attention? Are you challenged by his words? Have you become his disciple?

Jesus incites us. He is good, and he knows best. Learn from him.

God who reigns in the heavens, may I learn from you how to live. May I take your words seriously and tend to them, that they might transform and change my life. Amen.

7. A TEACHER WITH AUTHORITY

When Jesus had finished saying these things, the crowds were amazed at his teaching, because he taught as one who had authority, and not as their teachers of the law.

Matthew 7:28-29

During my college years, I was privileged to work as a personal assistant to a retired history professor who had received a "master teacher" distinction from the university administration. I picked up his laundry, shopped for his groceries, drove his car, and spent time watching him interact with former students, school officials, and dignitaries. Watching this man in action changed my life.

Though his specialty was the ancient Greek and Roman era, this professor had taken a special interest in the history of the university. He was often called to speak to alumni groups and historical societies, and he was a master storyteller. He could situate the listener on the old campus, depict with precision the personalities of past university presidents, and bring school history to life as though the listener was experiencing the moment as a student or bystander. No one spoke with a greater degree of authority on the history of the university. This inspired others to know more about the school and to love it.

Our reading today is found at the conclusion of the Sermon on the Mount, in Matthew 5–7. The people listening were amazed. Jesus told them to "love their enemies," to put away anger, contempt, and condemnation. He taught against the evils of lust and hatred and adultery. He gave instruction on generosity and prayer and service. He finished with a powerful analogy: "Therefore everyone who hears these words of mine and puts them into practice is like a wise man who built his house on the rock" (Matthew 7:24). When storms hit, nothing would sweep them away.

When we understand Jesus' teachings and begin applying them to our lives, our character is strengthened. During Jesus' time, the people observed that he possessed an authority that "the teachers of the law" did not. Jesus' words offered an immediate challenge to the status quo. To a degree greater than my college mentor, Jesus inspired his hearers to know more about God, to love God, and to live differently after an encounter with him.

Is there an area of your life that you would like Jesus to revolutionize? Write it in the space below. Pray for greater knowledge of God.

Lord, help me apply your teachings in the service of others. Amen.

8. LIVING WELL?

Then he called the crowd to him along with his disciples and said: "Whoever wants to be my disciple must deny themselves and take up their cross and follow me. For whoever wants to save their life will lose it, but whoever loses their life for me and for the gospel will save it. What good is it for someone to gain the whole world, yet forfeit their soul? Or what can anyone give in exchange for their soul?"

Mark 8:34-37

Not everyone watches the Super Bowl for the football game. Some watch for the commercials. During Super Bowl XLVII, an advertisement for a popular luxury automobile debuted. A young man sat down with Satan, who offered him a car. In his mind's eye, the young man was shown all the glories that would come with the car, all for the small price of his soul. The usual temptations dangled: beautiful women, wealth, and fame. The commercial ended humorously when a billboard was unveiled showing the cost of the automobile, which was well within his price range. The message to the consumer was plain: You can have this car, and all these things besides, and still retain your soul.

Or can you?

Marketing professionals often tap our need to define ourselves through possessions, in effect saying, "Your life will be complete and you will be happy if you own this, use this, eat this." Some of us are tempted by wealth and accumulation. Others are tempted by fame or success or sexual prowess. Yet Jesus is clear, saying, "Sure, you can gain all those things for the price of your soul. Is it worth the price?"

Most of us are not tempted to strike a bargain as dramatically as the man in the commercial. Instead, we experience a slow and prolonged slide, waking one day and wondering how our lives were spent so poorly. Jesus shocks us back to our senses, calling us to assess our lives. Jesus asks, "Are you taking up your cross? Are you following me? Are you losing your life for my sake and for the good news?"

Jesus asks us if *he* is our highest pursuit.

Where does he rank on your priority list?

God, may your grace set my heart upon you and your gospel above all else. In Christ's name. Amen.

9. A DIFFERENT TYPE OF REIGN

"For even the Son of Man did not come to be served, but to serve, and to give his life as a ransom for many."

Mark 10:45

One day, Jesus was traveling with his closest followers. Two of his disciples, James and John, approached and asked for the best seats in Jesus' kingdom on the day his reign began. If Jesus had been president, it would have been as if James had wanted to be vice president and John the secretary of state. Jesus told them they didn't know what they were asking. Further, they didn't understand what kind of king Jesus would be.

Overhearing the request, other disciples began quarreling over who among them was the greatest. They knew Jesus was great, and they assumed his greatness would propel their own fame and power.

Jesus knew he had a problem on his hands. The disciples were expecting him to come as an earthly leader, striking down enemies and accruing power, reigning with might and doling out justice. But Jesus' vision was different. He told his disciples, "Other kings might reign like that. But not me, and not you."

The disciples didn't get it. Too often, neither do we. We are not called to reign with power and might, like earthly kings. We are called to serve with Jesus, exercising a different type of power and demonstrating a different type of reign. In the end, Jesus laid down his life for us as a ransom, so that we in turn might lay down our lives in service to others. Jesus took on our nature so that we might put on his nature. He changes us by his love.

Once you grasp what Jesus was teaching, how might your life change? What would it mean to live a life of service to others? How can you serve your spouse, children, friends, and co-workers, in ways that give witness to Jesus' service for us?

It is one thing to know and another to do. Put Jesus' teaching into action.

Holy and loving God, you laid down your life for me. Jesus has shown me a different way—the way of service. May I humble myself, living as you have called. I ask these things in the name of Jesus. Amen.

10. TRUE NORTH

But seek first his kingdom and his righteousness, and all these things will be given to you as well.

Matthew 6:33

When I was a senior in high school, our church hosted a baccalaureate service for those approaching graduation. We all wore caps and gowns and processed in together. Church members understood that we were nearing a rite of passage, and they wanted to recognize that special moment. The service included a short message from the pastor. He chose Matthew 6 as his text and talked to us about life in God's kingdom. As a teenager, anxious about the future, I remember taking comfort in Jesus' instruction, "Do not worry about tomorrow, for tomorrow will worry about itself. Each day has enough trouble of its own" (Matthew 6:34). More profoundly, I remember finding a "true north" in Christ's teaching to "seek first the kingdom." I did not know what I was going to study, where I was going to work, or if I was going to be married. But I did know that if my life were lived for Jesus and his kingdom, everything else would work out.

Many of the decisions we make are based on what we believe is most important. What determines your course as you pass through life? What is your default value? It may be something that you grew up with, something your parents taught you directly or through example. Can you put your finger on it?

Now what would your life be like if you substituted something else as your highest value? What if it was Christ and his kingdom? What would change? What would be difficult? What would be better?

As we come to greater knowledge of God, our lives take on a new shape. We have new standards and new priorities. Sometimes the change is slow and tough. Sometimes the change is immediate and radical. Either way, the long-term result is remarkable. Rather than being self-centered, our concern is for the well-being of others. Instead of being angry, we have peace. Instead of being restless, we gain contentment.

C. S. Lewis put it well: "Aim at heaven and you will get earth 'thrown in': aim at earth and you will get neither."[3]

Lord, what am I truly seeking? Is it you? Or is my life determined by a different set of values? May I follow you in all things, whatever the cost. Amen.

Learning the Scriptures

11. REQUIRED READING

All Scripture is God-breathed and is useful for teaching, rebuking, correcting and training in righteousness, so that the servant of God may be thoroughly equipped for every good work.

2 Timothy 3:16-17

One of my favorite church programs is called Bible Drill. Children and youth are given passages from the Bible to memorize and are trained to locate any book of the Bible quickly. They learn all sixty-six books in their proper order and recite verses from memory for a panel of judges. Each year, adults find themselves amazed and inspired by the knowledge of these young people!

Biblical knowledge is valuable. It is indispensable for growth in holiness. But as a Bible Drill teacher, I was aware of the danger that students would come to regard the Bible only as a source of religious information, not as a means to know God. It is not enough for us to quote verses or find our way around the Bible; instead, we must encounter its source: God the Father, Son, and Holy Spirit.

The Bible has many uses. It teaches us, warns us concerning wrong behavior, guides us along better paths, and equips us to live blameless before God and other people. Then, by God's grace, we can do the good things God commands us to do, as a loving response to the God we know and an invitation to our neighbors to love God. To know God more fully and to live for him more faithfully, the Bible is required reading. Within it, we discover God's character and his purposes for humanity.

So where to begin? Dallas Willard once suggested that over the course of one year, it would be better for just ten verses of Scripture to get "into the substance of our lives" than for the entire Bible to flash before our eyes.[4]

Start with a well-known and beloved passage of Scripture, and dwell there a while. Romans 8, Psalm 23, or the Lord's Prayer (Matthew 6:9-13) are all excellent places to begin. A desire to know other books and passages of the Bible will soon follow. God will guide you to teachers and other resources as you have need.

As you grow in knowledge, the reward will be exceedingly great. Open your Bible. Listen for God.

Holy Spirit, guide me in all truth through the words of Scripture. Amen.

12. KNOW THE SOURCE

Above all, you must understand that no prophecy of Scripture came about by the prophet's own interpretation of things. For prophecy never had its origin in the human will, but prophets, though human, spoke from God as they were carried along by the Holy Spirit.

2 Peter 1:20-21

During the 2008 presidential election, Democratic candidate Barack Obama was widely praised for his engagement with the electorate through social media. Obama reached out to the public through Twitter, sharing updates from the campaign trail and offering voters an inside look at the workings of his staff. After he was elected president, his account fell silent until White House officials could outline suitable policies that would maintain the president's privacy and ensure safety. Several months later, updates resumed, coming from the president (rather than staffers) and denoted by his initials.

When we receive a message, we are always interested in the source. Just as we will interpret a Twitter message directly from the president differently than an update from a member of his staff, so too will we read the Bible differently when acknowledging a divine voice speaking through the human authors of Scripture. Knowing the message's origin will help determine our response.

In 2 Peter, we find an acknowledgment of God's divine speaking through certain people at key moments in time, bringing to us a message God intends for us to hear. Christians believe that God has spoken to us in and through the Bible, and we are called to listen. Granted, interpreting the message can be difficult, as the Bible itself admits (2 Peter 3:14-18). But generally, for those who diligently seek to understand these things, the principles found throughout Scripture are clear concerning God's power, justice, and love for his creation.

We should be both wise and humble in reading and interpreting the Bible, placing the proper weight on matters that are clearly established and maintaining generosity and charity on more minor matters of doctrine. The best interpreters of Scripture have maintained this balance throughout history, acknowledging the divine inspiration of the Bible while offering their best understandings, with love, for their readers.

When individuals are able to offer their interpretations of Scripture in love, they give witness to its source, the God who is love, and much more.

God, by your grace, help me hear your voice in Scripture. Amen.

13. A LIFE OF LEARNING

Do your best to present yourself to God as one approved, a worker who does not need to be ashamed and who correctly handles the word of truth.

2 Timothy 2:15

When I was a student in seminary, one of my teachers was a man whose course on Bible study methods was one of the most anticipated and beloved classes for the entire student body. Every single one of my friends and acquaintances in seminary named this professor as one of the most important figures in their theological education. He taught us to read carefully and well, and he instilled in us a humble confidence in interpreting the Bible. Most important, he taught us that keen observation and sound interpretation are not enough. Application of biblical truth is critical for our witness to Jesus Christ.

In 2 Timothy, Paul offers encouragement to a young pastor. Speaking from his experience as an apostle, leader, and church planter, Paul tells Timothy to have the confidence of one who has been "approved" and "who does not need to be ashamed" before God. Remembering our position before God is always a good first step for any action: we have been approved and accepted by God through Christ's love, which was demonstrated for us on the cross and confirmed by God in the resurrection. We don't need to be ashamed, for Christ took our shame and put it to death in his body (1 Peter 2:24; Hebrews 12:2). God loves us; we needn't have any doubt. That declaration has been made public.

In light of our approval by God, we are called to "correctly [handle] the word of truth." In presenting the testimony of Scripture and the person of Jesus Christ to others, we should strive for truthfulness. Disciples of Jesus are not only called to be believers, but learners. We are called to obtain knowledge and to pass that knowledge on to others.

My professor's greatest gift was not the experience he created in his classes. Rather, it was the tools he gave us to know God through Scripture. He enabled us to "[handle] the word of truth." Surround yourself with mentors who will do the same for you, who will enable you to know and understand the Bible, so that you may then better know, love, and serve God.

Lord, equip me with the skills I need to handle your truth faithfully. Amen.

14. A SHEPHERD'S PSALM

The LORD is my shepherd, I lack nothing.
He makes me lie down in green pastures,
he leads me beside quiet waters,
he refreshes my soul.
He guides me along the right paths
for his name's sake.

Psalm 23:1-3

Several years ago, I attended a seminar that focused on living everyday life as a disciple of Jesus. At the conclusion of the first day, the class was invited to pray the Twenty-third Psalm while going to sleep that night and be ready to discuss the experience the next morning.

At the beginning of the next session, people offered their reflections. It was amazing to hear the power those words had in the lives of my classmates. Many noted a felt presence or a strong sense of God's love. The discussion leader, smiling, told us that he normally fell asleep when the Lord made him lie down in green pastures. He said this is a perfectly acceptable response for people who are worn out and beaten down by the busyness of life. Sometimes, the first thing we need in order to grow closer to God is more sleep!

The Twenty-third Psalm, thought to be written by David, is an incredible resource for growing in knowledge of God. What does it teach us? The first three verses, shown above, are profound, offering four images that reshape our imaginations. First, we are told that the Lord is a "shepherd" who provides for the well-being of the sheep. David says, "I lack nothing."

The second and third images are "green pastures" and "quiet waters" that bring rest and refreshment. Here, the sheep are nourished and restored, safe from any threat. Quiet waters ensure that predators can be heard; lying down suggests freedom from danger. God's kingdom is secure, never in trouble.

Fourth is the image of "right paths." God has a way for us to walk, and he will lead and direct us. He does this for his glory, inviting us alongside him as companions. There will much to learn along the way. Perhaps there will be travail, as we will see later in this psalm, but we will triumph in the end. Our future is sure with God.

Meditate on these words today. Carry them with you. Commit them to memory. Ask God to teach you.

Almighty God, I wish to know you and to live in your kingdom, trusting you to keep me safe and to lead me, as a shepherd guides the sheep. Amen.

15. NEVER SHAKEN

Even though I walk
*   through the darkest valley,*
I will fear no evil,
*   for you are with me;*
your rod and your staff,
*   they comfort me.*
You prepare a table before me
*   in the presence of my enemies.*
You anoint my head with oil;
*   my cup overflows.*
Surely your goodness and love will follow me
*   all the days of my life,*
and I will dwell in the house of the LORD
*   forever.*

Psalm 23:4-6

If you've ever faced a difficult season, these words of the psalmist will resonate. The darkest valley, a cup overflowing, a head anointed with oil, a feast with enemies present, an eternal dwelling place, goodness and love—these are powerful images. Psalm 23 is commonly read at funerals. In the span of six verses, this Scripture acknowledges the pain and challenges of life while professing and clinging to hope. Despite hardship, confidence in God is never shaken.

These words have been tried and tested. But is God really like this? Can God really be trusted in the face of evil? When our world collapses and we find ourselves under attack, is God truly with us? The psalmist says yes.

Think of your own experience and ponder these questions: what if God's goodness was beyond anything you could ever fathom? What if God offered you a sure hand during your most difficult trial? What if you could stake your life on an eternal hope, made real and assured in the life, death, resurrection, and reign of Jesus? True knowledge of God comes not only through classes or sermons, but also through experience. God has invited us to a relationship through Jesus. We are invited to become disciples of Jesus, to trust him as the very best. And he will teach us, by the power of the Holy Spirit. We will come to know his Father, experiencing God as children experience the love of a parent. Through that knowledge, we will be made new.

If you are new to Christianity, Psalm 23 is an excellent initiation into the life of God's eternal kingdom. If you have long known God, you have confirmed these truths by experience. Continue in the way, and anticipate what God will bring.

Good and beautiful God, I am thankful that you will walk with me in good times and bad, and that you will lead me to dwell with you eternally. Amen.

Session Four

Studying the Scriptures

16. HAVING THE MIND OF CHRIST

The person with the Spirit makes judgments about all things, but such a person is not subject to merely human judgments, for,

> *"Who has known the mind of the Lord
>   so as to instruct him?"*

But we have the mind of Christ.

1 Corinthians 2:15-16

During my time as a graduate student at the University of Kansas, I would gather with classmates to prepare for tests or final exams. We would compare notes and review assigned readings. The information covered in each course was pertinent, but so were the style and personality of the instructor. We would ask, "What will this teacher look for? What are the likely questions? What's on the teacher's mind?" Our relationship with the instructor would help us to analyze the information and make an educated guess concerning what would appear on the test.

Paul writes that, in a similar way, Christians have the "mind of Christ." What does this mean? The difference is one of degree, and it is significant. Those in Christ not only make guesses regarding what God might think; we are able to know God's mind on matters of importance for the life of faith.

Through the study of Scripture, we gain familiarity with what God is like. With the help of the Christian tradition and sound reason, we come to know and understand God's character. We learn that God is all knowing, all-powerful, all good, and much more. Concerning our ethics, we are given instruction on how to live. In the Scriptures we find vital information about God that shapes and reshapes our patterns of thought. In Romans 12:2, Paul writes, "Do not conform to the pattern of this world, but be transformed by the renewing of your mind. Then you will be able to test and approve what God's will is—his good, pleasing and perfect will."

Therefore, study is a vital practice for every Christian. Ask a pastor or trusted Christian friend for books that might help you grow, or consider listening to audio recordings of knowledgeable pastors or theologians on your commute to and from work or school. Pray, asking God to help you separate truth from falsehood. Let the truth renew your mind, so that you might have the mind of Christ.

Lord, place in me a desire to study Scripture, that I might come to have your mind. Amen.

17. A GENTLE ANSWER

But in your hearts revere Christ as Lord. Always be prepared to give an answer to everyone who asks you to give the reason for the hope that you have. But do this with gentleness and respect.

1 Peter 3:15

I am a parent of two young children. My daughter is now three and has begun to say and do all kinds of wild things. From time to time, she will do or say something I find remarkable. Sometimes she will display the wisdom only children possess. Sometimes she will do or say something wrong. In each case I ask her, "Why did you do or say that?"

Because she is three years old, she does not always know why, or is not able to articulate her reasons. For those of us who have placed our faith in Christ, we know what that feels like. In some matters of faith, we are like children. We do and say things we do not understand.

In today's Scripture, however, we are called to reason through our belief and practice. There's a very simple purpose for this: when others ask us why we do or say things, we can offer a reasonable explanation. We are called to possess a knowledge of God that we can share, not as slick rhetoricians or arrogant blowhards but as gentle and respectful witnesses.

In some circles, Christians are thought to be self-righteous and cocksure, bullies who pressure others to accept their version of the truth. If you have suffered at the hands of such people, I tell you on behalf of all Christians that I am sorry. There is a better way, modeled with excellence by many Christians throughout history and even today. I have been blessed to know some of these people. I hope you will come to know Christ, thereby adding to the number of those humble witnesses who know what they believe and respectfully share their reasons with others.

Of course, reaching that goal will require work. But Jesus will meet you where you are and carry you forth as you are called. In fact, you are already on the way! Ask him for help, and surely he will teach you.

Jesus, you are my teacher and I am your student. Help me to learn your ways, so that I may answer anyone who asks about my life in you. Give me words that point to your grace. Amen.

18. A VISION ADJUSTMENT

Open my eyes that I may see
wonderful things in your law.

Psalm 119:18

"Law" has a bad rap.

Oftentimes, when people speak of God's commandments, they imagine a divine killjoy, a cosmic being who enjoys placing limits on his creatures. But the Bible does not speak of "law" in this way. Instead, law is seen as evidence of God's grace, a sign that God cares for the created order. If we view the commands in Scripture negatively, we may need a vision adjustment.

Consider a goldfish. In order to thrive, the goldfish must be placed within a suitable habitat. The bowl must contain water that is clean. A small plant or rock provides coverage or a place to hide in the event the fish perceives danger. Food must be provided. The water must be changed periodically, to purify the environment.

It is the same with God's commands. The purpose of the law is not solely to restrict human freedom, but to place reasonable boundaries on human society that will lead to the flourishing of the whole. Lawmakers and those in the justice system know that good laws, fairly enacted and enforced, make life better for all people. When wrongs are committed, there is jurisprudence and fair verdicts. Good laws give stability through a public standard of fairness and judicial process. They provide a healthy environment within which individuals may prosper.

The psalmist prays, "Open my eyes that I may see wonderful things in your law." As we study the Bible, we should recall this prayer. When the Bible offers a command, we should not be quick to judge or dismiss what it is teaching. Instead, we should ask why the command is being offered and how it should be observed today. This should be done with prayer and careful discernment. Our highest law should always be Christ, who is the fulfillment of the law. Jesus himself teaches us how we understand and apply God's law.

The commands of Scripture are given for our good. Study them, and take them to heart.

Merciful God, teach me your commands, and help me to see them as an evidence of your love for all people. Help me to discern, in community with others, how we are to live according to your instruction. In Jesus' name. Amen.

19. THE NEW BIRTH

Jesus replied, "Very truly I tell you, no one can see the kingdom of God unless they are born again."

John 3:3

Being "born again" has come to be associated with a particular form of religious experience. There is a feeling or emotion, a prayer spoken quietly under one's breath, a testimony that Jesus has "come into my heart." For some, this is a valid and truthful account of the beginnings of their Christian life. But for others, this experience is elusive. Careful thinking about "birth" might be in order.

Everyone is born, but not all births are the same. Some follow prolonged labor. Others progress rapidly, though not without pain. But all births culminate in a change, a difference in status, functioning, and social relations. After the cord is cut, the child begins a new way of being. The parent, too, begins a new way of investing in the life of the child.

As someone of Baptist heritage, my birth in Christ was rapid. My wife, Molly, experienced a slow awakening to God's grace in the Methodist tradition, but in retrospect she can see moments when God turned her life decisively for divine purposes. As a result, in my family we have two very different accounts of being "born again." But we have no doubt that in both, God was at work. How is God at work in your life? Do you recall a moment of rapid initiation into life with God? Or was your experience slow, measured, and steady?

Or have you yet to have such an experience of Jesus Christ?

If it is the former, tell your story to someone over coffee or a meal. If it is the latter, ask God to reveal himself to you. Investigate Jesus in the way Nicodemus did, as we read in John 3. Ask the questions Nicodemus asked, and listen to the answers Jesus gave. Listen for God.

God's love for you is constant. That's just the way God is. But God may be enacting a change in your inner being, assuring you of his grace and inviting you to discipleship. Pay attention. Be mindful. Life in God's kingdom awaits.

Holy Spirit, change my heart, and awaken me to the grace of God given in Christ Jesus, so that I might live a new life with you. Amen.

20. GOD'S GREAT LOVE

For God so loved the world that he gave his one and only Son,
that whoever believes in him shall not perish but have eternal life.
John 3:16

In the 1970s and 1980s, a man named Rollen Stewart traveled the country and appeared on countless American sports telecasts, wearing a rainbow wig and holding a large sign that said John 3:16. Stewart's story is one of grace and folly. He was far from a perfect man. But after meeting Jesus, he was driven to spread the message of God's love, which he thought was captured best in John 3:16.

Similarly, during the 2009 BCS National Championship game in college football, Florida quarterback Tim Tebow wore eye black referencing this verse of Scripture. Once this marking was shown on television, "John 3:16" soared to the top of Google's search results. Tebow communicated a message, and many viewers responded.

So what does the verse mean? If it's so important, what difference does it make for us?

Let's consider what the verse actually says. The writer of John's Gospel makes several tremendous claims. First, "God so loved the world." God's love is all encompassing in scope and is directed toward all creation. God's love is for the world and all it contains. Second, "he gave his one and only Son." Just as we express our love for someone through bestowal of a gift, God gave the unique gift of himself in the person of his Son. The gift was costly, irreplaceable, and unrepeatable; the greatest gift ever given.

Third, "whoever believes in him shall not perish but have eternal life." Death, sooner or later, will come for us all. But because we are God's treasures, whom he loves, God does not give us up to death. We are called to believe in Jesus, who promises eternal life not only in the future but starting today. "I have come that they may have life," said Jesus, "and have it to the full" (John 10:10). What do we make of these claims? How do they change us? They mean that God loves us beyond our wildest imaginings; loves you. Respond by believing in Jesus. His love will spring up in you like living water (John 4:14).

You will be a new person. That, truly, will change the world.

Loving God, you have not abandoned us, but have made a way for us to know your grace. May I trust in your Son. Amen.

A Study of Christian Ethics

21. THE GREATEST COMMANDMENT

Jesus replied: "'Love the Lord your God with all your heart and with all your soul and with all your mind.' This is the first and greatest commandment. And the second is like it: 'Love your neighbor as yourself.' All the Law and the Prophets hang on these two commandments."

Matthew 22:37-40

I have been the driver on many church trips. I even drove a school bus for a few years. Whenever I had a new crew of passengers, I would explain the rules. Rule number one: do not distract the driver. Most of the other rules stemmed from this one; in my universe, it was the greatest commandment.

One day, when Jesus was teaching a crowd, a religious leader approached and asked a good question. "Teacher," he said, "which is the greatest commandment?" As an observant Jew, Jesus had a long list of laws to choose from: 613, to be exact. For his answer, he went to the heart of the law, leaning on Deuteronomy 6:5 and Leviticus 19:18. "Love God," Jesus said. "Love your neighbor." In his universe (and it is his), that's the greatest commandment.

Knowing God means living in right relationship with God and with others. Your ethics should reflect your association with God. The closer the resemblance, the greater the evidence of intimacy. When others gaze upon your life and measure your decisions, they should see something of God. This is called giving witness.

One of the things that made Jesus so remarkable was his integrity. When Jesus gave his answer about the greatest commandment, he placed himself squarely in the court of public opinion. Did Jesus meet his own standard? Did he love God? Did he love his neighbor?

The greatest evidence is seen on the cross. Jesus so loved his Father that he became obedient to the point of death, securing our salvation by atoning for our sin (Philippians 2:5-11). Jesus so loved us that he died for us, "while we were yet sinners" (Romans 5:8 KJV). There is no greater example of love and integrity.

Jesus intends for us to follow his way. He will train us to obey the greatest commandment. Trust Jesus. He will lead the way.

Lord Jesus, your teaching is wise and perfect. Guide me in your ways, help me obey all you have commanded, and give me power by your Holy Spirit. Amen.

22. GOD SHOWS THE WAY

He has shown you, O mortal, what is good.
   And what does the LORD require of you?
To act justly and to love mercy
   and to walk humbly with your God.

Micah 6:8

I grew up going fishing with my dad. Starting with a Snoopy rod and reel, I practiced my release in the backyard, casting with a rubber weight on the end of my line. Before heading out on the open water, we spent time at my great-grandmother's farm, pulling fish out of a small pond. I was taught to be careful around hooks and mindful of surroundings when directing the rod. The more time I spent with my dad fishing, the more I learned, either through instruction or example. My dad showed the way.

In the book of Micah, the people of Israel are given a very simple reminder of something they had been shown: the way of life with God. What is required of us? Justice. Mercy. Humble companionship with God. But just as it is with fishing, these things take practice and are often enhanced through guidance from others who are more knowledgeable and more highly skilled.

In the Bible, true religion is always found in the coalescence of belief and action, professed faith and a demonstrated integrity.

God demands this. Not only are we expected to say the right things or to profess the right doctrines; we are expected to do the right things, enacting justice and mercy.

It's more challenging than you might think. To live life well before God, your knowledge is constantly put to the test. You are required to grow and learn, to examine your assumptions, to filter them through the lens of faith. Sometimes you will find you are not living as God requires. Through Scripture and prayer, your view of what is right might change. Knowledge of God will reframe your understandings of justice, mercy, and humility. It's a growth process.

A true understanding of justice and mercy will drive you back to the cross of Jesus, where both are seen: God's perfect justice enacted against sin, and his abundant mercy made manifest for all people. Jesus' display of humility will in turn humble you. Jesus shows the way.

Lord, teach me what is right. May I grow in knowledge of your truth and live according to the path you have shown me. In Jesus' name. Amen.

23. DO GOOD

For it is God's will that by doing good you should silence the ignorant talk of foolish people.

1 Peter 2:15

Though we might like it to be otherwise, following Jesus leads to persecution and hardship and trouble. If we're really following Jesus, we are going to encounter the "ignorant talk of foolish people" referred to in today's Scripture. Skeptics will scoff, haters will hate, the proud will mock. Your best and most godly response: "doing good."

What does doing good look like? It takes many forms. We have three widows on our street, and when a storm in Kansas City recently left us with a foot of snow, my wife called to make sure they were okay. A number of people in our church have adopted children, taking in orphans. My mother-in-law travels to show mercy to the people of Haiti and Honduras. I know of a group in Texas who for many years visited poor communities in Mexico to conduct eye exams and provide free glasses. This past Christmas, by God's grace, our church collected $1.25 million for AIDS relief in Africa.

If people want to dismiss Christians, they can. But if you look closely, you'll find many believers quietly doing good. It may take the form of a school worker sanitizing desks and mopping floors to maintain a clean environment for the students. It may be a banker who, honoring God through the stewardship of money, is honest in dealings and fair in lending practices. It might be a Boy Scout helping an elderly person across the street, not for the badge but because of a love for God. Surely you can think of many more examples.

Instead of just talking about doing good things, take action. Get a few friends together. Follow John Wesley's admonition to "do all the good you can." Put your heads together and generate some ideas. Then get to work.

When people ask why you're doing it, tell them it's in the name of Christ. Some people may quickly change the subject. But others may find themselves intrigued. Either way, love everyone and keep doing good.

God, help me to know you and to do the good you command. In Christ's name. Amen.

24. JOINING THE MISSION

"The Spirit of the Lord is on me,
because he has anointed me
to proclaim good news to the poor.
He has sent me to proclaim freedom for the prisoners
and recovery of sight for the blind,
to set the oppressed free,
to proclaim the year of the Lord's favor."

Luke 4:18-19

One of the most famous speeches in American history is Abraham Lincoln's Second Inaugural Address.[5] Lincoln opened with remarks concerning the state of the union, making reference to the Civil War and the conditions that led to its outbreak. The speech is notable for its brevity and clarity, but also for Lincoln's use of theology in the public square. Lincoln recognized that citizens of both North and South "read the same Bible and pray to the same God, and each invokes His aid against the other." Lincoln went further, saying "the prayers of both could not be answered" and that "neither has been answered fully." In this instance, Lincoln allowed for the mystery of God's providence, but he concluded, "If God wills that it continue until all the wealth piled by the bondsman's two hundred and fifty years of unrequited toil shall be sunk, and until every drop of blood drawn with the lash shall be paid by another drawn with the sword, as was said three thousand years ago, so still it must be said 'the judgments of the Lord are true and righteous altogether.'" In the speech, Lincoln's convictions are firm; his direction resolute. The Union would be preserved; freedom would prevail.

In a small synagogue in Nazareth long ago, Jesus likewise gave an address, naming his convictions and direction. In Luke 4, Jesus walked to the front of the room and took up the Isaiah scroll. As was the custom, he chose his words carefully, picking what those gathered needed to hear. When he finished reading, he said, "Today this Scripture is fulfilled in your hearing" (v. 21). He sat down, and his meaning was plain: Jesus was the one to fulfill these words. It was his mission.

In Christ, we are called to join that mission: to bring good news to the poor, freedom to the captives, sight to the blind, relief to the oppressed, and the announcement of God's favor for all.

Are you following the leader?

Jesus, life in your kingdom is good news. Help me to be an agent of your purposes. Amen.

25. A CROSS-SHAPED LIFE

As a prisoner for the Lord, then, I urge you to live a life worthy of the calling you have received. Be completely humble and gentle; be patient, bearing with one another in love.

Ephesians 4:1-2

For certain careers and vocations, we have expectations for behavior that are expressed in pledges or oaths. Doctors and nurses pledge to "prescribe regimens for the good of my patients according to my ability and my judgment and never do harm to anyone." Police officers promise to "never betray . . . the public trust." The president of the United States pledges to "preserve, protect and defend the Constitution of the United States."[6]

Our callings give shape to our lives. The life of a Christian is no different. Once Jesus has joined your life to his, you are expected to live a certain way. The oath of the Christian might be as simple as "Jesus is Lord," but the implications are far-reaching. They touch every dimension of your life.

How are you called to live? As Paul writes in Ephesians, you should be "humble and gentle." You should be "patient, bearing with one another in love." But in order to be these things, you have to begin training. You must be a disciple. You must learn from

Jesus, and from others more advanced in the way of Christ, how your life can take on this shape, the shape of the cross.

Bible study and prayer are two essential practices. Worship is the heart of spiritual formation. There are other practices as well, such as fasting and serving and seeking solitude. One does not grow in Christlikeness without intentionality and purpose. Do you wish to grow? Do you wish to become a person more at peace, more generous, more loving?

Then go to a respected pastor or a friend who is farther along the path. Ask for help. Outline a curriculum. Take up daily practices that God, by grace, may use to transform your character.

If you desire to be like Jesus, then God is already at work. As you exercise obedience to his calling, God will be with you on the way, guiding each step.

God, even if my life is a wreck, you can put it back together and make it beautiful, redeemed. Make me new. Amen.

The Person and Work of the Holy Spirit

26. THE MORE YOU KNOW

I have not stopped giving thanks for you, remembering you in my prayers. I keep asking that the God of our Lord Jesus Christ, the glorious Father, may give you the Spirit of wisdom and revelation, so that you may know him better.

Ephesians 1:16-17

On October 2, 2006, the Amish community near Nickel Mines, Pennsylvania, experienced a horrendous tragedy. A lone gunman entered a one-room schoolhouse and fired on ten girls, killing five. He then shot himself. The Amish people were tremendously grieved, but to the public's astonishment they forgave the shooter. The community then donated money to the killer's widow and three children. In a world of skepticism and doubt, the Amish community gave witness to a more hopeful reality, the kingdom of God.

To forgive someone under such circumstances shows a radical understanding of grace. For the Amish, the repudiation of vengeance and retaliatory violence is grounded in the cross of Jesus Christ. On the cross, Jesus offered forgiveness to those who were killing him and secured the forgiveness of sin for all who would subsequently place their faith in him. What the Amish knew about Jesus was the basis for their action—not the romantic ideal of forgiveness but its historical reality.

In Ephesians 1, Paul offers a powerful prayer: "that the God of our Lord Jesus Christ, the glorious Father, may give you the Spirit of wisdom and revelation, so that you might know him better." Paul prays for knowledge. He does not wish for his hearers to speculate about God, but to know God and to live according to such knowledge.

In the life of the Christian, it is the Spirit of God that leads us to greater knowledge of God. This includes a growing familiarity with the person and work of God, but also includes a deeper understanding of self. The Spirit of God confronts our sin, unearths our imperfections, and helps us face them. When we read the Bible, listen to a sermon, or consider a devotion like this one, we should ask the Spirit of God to teach us, to lead us to truth.

As we know God better, we will learn to love our enemies, pray for those who persecute us, and offer radical forgiveness as the Amish Christians did.

Holy Spirit, lead me to greater knowledge of you. Amen.

27. INSIDE-OUT RENEWAL

"This is the covenant I will make with the people of Israel
after that time," declares the LORD.
"I will put my law in their minds
and write it on their hearts.
I will be their God,
and they will be my people."

Jeremiah 31:33

Our family recently took on a home remodeling project. In our bathroom, a portion of the tile around our tub had begun to decay. That was the first sign of trouble. We investigated further. Upon touch, the wall sank backward. We had a major problem.

Next was demolition. It took a lot of work to remove the tiling, cut and carry out our cast-iron tub, and discover the root of the problem. Soon it became clear: A beveled edge beneath the tile was made of plywood. When moisture had penetrated the grout, the boards had become moist, and rot had followed. Under it all, a portion of our floorboard had fallen through.

You might say we had a character problem. The integrity of our materials had failed, corruption had set in, and there was only one way forward. We had to pull out the rotten stuff, bring in the new, and restore what we could. And we did it.

And God does it.

In the book of Jeremiah, we read of God's promise to put his law into the minds and hearts of his people. But we have a character problem. Our integrity has failed, corruption has set in, and there is only one way forward. Jesus sends us the Holy Spirit to pull out the rotten stuff, bring in the new, and restore us, making us whole. We trust God to do it.

Whether you are at the beginning, middle, or end of your day, take a few moments to reflect on your life. Where are you struggling or broken? Where do you need help? Where does your character need refinement? What do you read in Scripture that connects with you? Write those things down. Ask God for help. Listen for the Spirit.

God's new covenant, ratified in Christ, carries the promise of a different kind of life. Trust the Spirit of God to bring it close to your heart and mind.

Father in heaven, transform my character so that I naturally fulfill your commands. Fill me with the Spirit. Amen.

28. EVERYONE'S IN

"And afterward,
   I will pour out my Spirit on all people.
Your sons and daughters will prophesy,
   your old men will dream dreams,
   your young men will see visions."

Joel 2:28

When I was a kid, it was common for classmates to begin a game and then close the circle. Only certain people were allowed to play. If it was boys, girls were out. If it was girls, boys were out. If it was the cool kids, "less cool" kids were excluded. Lines were drawn. Those with power used their gifts or savvy to draw boundaries and maintain them.

We may believe this is true in the Christian life. Some people are close to God. They hear God speaking; we can't. They say God "opened a door" and gave direction; we wander, lost. We want to belong but, lacking experience, assume we've been left out.

In Joel's day there were people on the fringe, longing for the Spirit of God. If you read the Old Testament, you will see the Spirit of God resting on certain people, at certain times, for certain purposes. The Spirit was at work in the world, though seemingly not always with God's people. But Joel made a bold pronouncement: the day was coming when the Spirit would be with everyone in God's family. No more "he's in; she's out." Everyone's in.

In Acts 2, Peter quotes Joel to announce that that day has come. In Christ, everyone is on a level plane. The Spirit is given to all who believe—men and women, young and old. The Spirit isn't the possession of an upper religious tier. It isn't bestowed on a special, select few. It isn't dolloped on a charismatic leader, only for a pivotal moment. It is given to all God's people, all the time.

If you have received Christ, the Spirit of God is dwelling within you and working to change your heart. That means when you pray, the Spirit prays with you (Romans 8:26). When you need help, the Spirit gives guidance (John 16:13). When you have a question, the Spirit is there to teach (John 14:26).

Trust the Holy Spirit. You're in.

Spirit, when I am confused, give me wisdom. When I am lost, give me direction. When I am down, bring me joy. May I know you are always with me. Amen.

29. THE SAME SPIRIT

When all the people were being baptized, Jesus was baptized too. And as he was praying, heaven was opened and the Holy Spirit descended on him in bodily form like a dove. And a voice came from heaven: "You are my Son, whom I love; with you I am well pleased."

Luke 3:21-22

Spending an afternoon on the playground with my daughter can be an enlightening experience. I'm twice her height, but she invites me to crawl through tunnels and climb on equipment designed for someone her size. I do my best to tag along, look at the world from her perspective, and experience solidarity with her by living life, however briefly, as she does.

Some people have a hard time believing that God identifies with us, understands us, and can therefore help us. But in Luke 3, while all the people are being baptized, Jesus is baptized too, showing solidarity with us in a way that far exceeds anything I attempt while playing with my daughter.

The sinless one goes into the waters, shoulder to shoulder with those present. The Spirit descends, and a voice from heaven proclaims love and delight for the "Son," implying divine parentage.

In Jesus' ministry, he refers to God as "Father." At his baptism, we may conclude that it is God the Father who speaks.

We have noted already that in baptism, Jesus identifies with us and invites us to follow his example. Further, we see that the Spirit, descending on Jesus, foreshadows Jesus' sending of the Spirit to his disciples, equipping them for mission and ministry in the world (John 20:21-22). The Father, announcing pleasure in the Son, has likewise adopted those in Christ as "co-heirs," sons and daughters in the kingdom of the heavens (Romans 8:17).

Now, the Holy Spirit is available to us. The Spirit teaches us that in Jesus, God knows and understands every dimension of human experience. The Spirit affirms us, assuring us of the love of the Father.

God is personal and can be known. When we learn about God, we are not studying for an exam. We are growing in relationship with the One in whom we find our true home. Augustine said it best: "God has made us for himself and our hearts are restless until they find their rest in thee."[7]

Jesus, through faith I have received the Holy Spirit. Draw near to me, that I might draw near to you and find rest. Amen.

30. BE BOLD

When the day of Pentecost came, they were all together in one place. Suddenly a sound like the blowing of a violent wind came from heaven and filled the whole house where they were sitting. They saw what seemed to be tongues of fire that separated and came to rest on each of them. All of them were filled with the Holy Spirit and began to speak in other tongues as the Spirit enabled them.

Acts 2:1-4

I've been fortunate to have had a few experiences when I knew God was present, at work and active. I have had rich, deep conversations with close friends, together seeking God's will. There have been worship meetings where I knew God was glorified. I have served the poor and marginalized and felt it was Jesus himself we had helped. In each of these instances, I'm sure that the Spirit focused my vision, amplified my hearing, and directed my steps.

In Acts 2, fifty days following Jesus' death, a large number of disciples gathered in Jerusalem, "together." The festival of Pentecost had begun. Many foreigners had come to worship God. Suddenly there was action, described as a loud sound "like the blowing of a violent wind," filling the place they had gathered. As the disciples surveyed the room, "they saw what seemed to be tongues of fire that separated and came to rest on each of them."

The scene is visceral, the language imprecise ("like"; "what seemed to be"). What followed was as miraculous as it was revolutionary. Ordinary people, like you and me, were filled with the Holy Spirit and began to preach to everyone about Jesus. There was no language barrier. And people began to profess Jesus as the Christ.

What God did on that day, God does today. Like the earliest disciples, we receive the Holy Spirit and are given power to live as God commands, sharing the good news with others. Do not be afraid, for God is with you. As you grow in knowledge of God, be bold in telling others about what you have learned. Along the way, be open to new lessons.

Ask the Spirit to guide you, to give you words to say, so that others might see the goodness of God.

God, as I grow in knowledge of you, fill me with your Spirit, that I might tell others about you. In Jesus' name. Amen.

Loving God

The Nature of God

1. WHAT IS GOD LIKE?

And so we know and rely on the love God has for us. God is love.
Whoever lives in love lives in God, and God in them.

1 John 4:16

Several years ago, I had a conversation with someone on matters of theology and church leadership. We were discussing a new initiative and were trying to look at it from a number of different angles. This was a person I did not know very well. At the end of our time together, my conversation partner said, "Well, that wasn't as bad I thought it would be." My reputation had preceded me, I suppose. My friend's remark suggested that he expected me to take a critical approach, maybe even to be rough. In fact, the conversation was pleasant and constructive.

When we learn about someone new, we ask, "What is he or she like?" It is a natural first question. We want to know if the person is kind, generous, or joyful; mean-spirited, sarcastic, or jealous. We use words to capture character, and in establishing a reputation we convey that character to others. When we meet someone ourselves, what we have heard is either validated or corrected by way of our experience.

In a way, it's the same with God. We want to know what God is like. Knowing this is helpful, first for our own understanding and then for our relationship with God. Our ideas about God are vital for our spiritual growth. Knowing that God is love is a tremendous first step. The belief that God can be trusted and seeks good for us is much better than the alternative: if you believe that God is malicious and out to get us, the relationship won't go very far. Thankfully, we know that God is love, not because it sounds better but because we see God's love for us in the cross of Jesus Christ, who redeems us through his death and resurrection.

Knowing that God is love is only a beginning, but it is quite a beginning! Over time, you will come to possess an entire vocabulary when speaking about God. As your understanding deepens, so too will your relationship with God, enabling you to better serve God's purposes in the world.

Lord, help me to know you as love, that I might grow closer to you. Direct my steps, so that I might walk your paths. Amen.

2. BETTER THAN BBQ

Now this is eternal life: that they know you, the only true God, and Jesus Christ, whom you have sent.

John 17:3

When I was a college student, there was a barbecue place my close friends told me was unparalleled. A handful of these friends made an annual pilgrimage there—it was a several hours' drive from campus and only opened seasonally. Despite repeated urgings, I never made the trip, even though my friends raved over the experience and constantly urged me to join them. I was always too busy, or uninterested, or felt there were better ways to spend the time.

Eternal life is better than barbecue. But more often than not, we regard the offer as I did a chance to savor the finest pulled-pork sandwich my home state had to offer. Perhaps we are too busy, or uninterested, or think there are better ways to spend our days. Maybe we think the offer is too good to be true.

But it isn't. God loved us so much that he put on flesh in Jesus the Son. By coming to know Jesus, we come to know God. The life we then lead with Jesus becomes the best kind of life we could possibly want—partaking in God's grace, working to bring about healing and restoration, hope and redemption in a world that is bruised and broken. Who would pass that up?

We would, often because our imaginations are too small. But once we have obtained a glimpse of God and God's kingdom, nothing should keep us away. The barbecue joint I passed on would have cost a few hours in a car and a handful of dollars for a plate of meat. The reward would have been a full stomach and an experience worth remembering.

With Jesus, the cost is a little different. We are called to turn our lives over to him; he purchased us with his life. But the reward is much greater, and it is nothing less than eternal life.

What would it be like to dwell with God forever? At the heart of God's nature is a love so deep that God would go to any length to dwell with us eternally. Rather than thinking we have to chase after eternal life, it has come chasing after us.

Will you turn and receive it?

Jesus, I want the eternal life you offer. May I come to know and love you through this study. In your name I ask. Amen.

3. WITNESSES

There was a man sent from God whose name was John. He came
as a witness to testify concerning that light, so that through him
all might believe. He himself was not the light; he came only as a
witness to the light.

John 1:6-8

In 2007, Nike launched an advertising campaign centered on basketball phenom LeBron James, then of the Cleveland Cavaliers. A single word was prominent: witness. The basic message was that LeBron James is a talent unlike anything you have ever seen. By aligning yourself with LeBron, buying his jersey, or cheering him on, you are part of the moment and part of history. You are a witness, and you should invite others to be witnesses.

In our Scripture reading we encounter a witness. His name was John.

John the Baptist trusted that God would stick to his promises. The prophets had foretold the coming of a messiah, and John was called to pave the way. After retreating to the wilderness, John returned to preach a message of repentance and preparation for God's anointed.

John called all who heard him to prepare for the messiah, the one who would point the world, once again, to God and God's purposes. When Jesus finally arrived on the scene, John said, "Look, the Lamb of God, who takes away the sin of the world!" (John 1:29).

Like John, we are called to be witnesses. Once we have seen Jesus, we are called to tell other people about him. Unlike Nike's endless hype of LeBron James, in Jesus we have a hero whose star will never fade. And we have so much to celebrate. In Jesus, we announce the one who reveals God's nature to us through his healing touch, compassion, and wise teaching. Further, Christians claim God is revealed in Jesus' death and his resurrection. In Jesus, we discover what God is like.

Look upon Jesus, "the light." As you come to know him, seek faithfulness to him, as a witness. Invite others to consider who he is, what he is like, and how we might know him. In this way, you will be like John, a faithful servant pointing others to God.

God, through the person of Jesus teach me what you are like. Equip me as a faithful witness, changing my character so that others might see you at work in me. Amen.

4. FITTING TRIBUTE

For great is your love toward me . . .
you, Lord, are a compassionate and gracious God,
*   slow to anger, abounding in love and faithfulness.*

Psalm 86:13*a*, 15

An epitaph is an inscription found on a tombstone telling us something about the person buried beneath it. Mathematician Ludolph van Ceulen, the first person to calculate the number pi, was so proud of his achievement that he asked to have the number written to thirty-five digits above his grave. Author and radio host Studs Terkel, who spent much of his career talking to average people and exploring a wide range of subjects, rests below a headstone that reads, "Curiosity did not kill this cat." Comedian Spike Milligan's epitaph was written in Gaelic at the insistence of the church, so the humor is lost on many visitors. Translated, it reads, "I told you I was ill."[8]

When I was in seminary, one of my teachers invited his students to write their own epitaphs. The challenge was simple: Strive to live a life true to how you want to be remembered. But rising to that challenge is the difficult part.

In Psalm 86 we learn God is "compassionate and gracious . . . slow to anger, abounding in love and faithfulness." We also find these words in Exodus 34:6; Numbers 14:18; Nehemiah 9:31; Psalm 103:8; and elsewhere in Scripture. There are countless allusions similarly representing God's character. The writers of Scripture found these words to be true of God and recounted them often. And what God has been in the past, he can be counted on for in the future.

As you live your life with God, you will find the words from Scripture to be trustworthy and true. When you stumble, fall, make mistakes, and sin, you'll find that God's anger is slow and God's grace is overwhelming. Every time you consider the cross, you will discover this anew. When you see God's nature as the psalmist does, the results might be surprising. You'll find that you treat others likewise, and God's life will start to come through in yours.

God's love changes us. For that, we give God thanks.

God, help me to know you as "gracious and compassionate . . . slow to anger and abounding in love and faithfulness." Help me to experience this in my own life. Then change me from the inside out. Amen.

5. THE GREATEST LOVE

No, in all these things we are more than conquerors through him who loved us. For I am convinced that neither death nor life, neither angels nor demons, neither the present nor the future, nor any powers, neither height nor depth, nor anything else in all creation, will be able to separate us from the love of God that is in Christ Jesus our Lord.

Romans 8:37-39

You certainly have heard love songs that capture the depth of affection one person has for another. These songs use vivid language, such as "I Will Follow Him" by 1960s pop singer Little Peggy March; or more recently, the similarly titled "I Will Follow You into the Dark" by alt-rock band Death Cab for Cutie. For country fans, you might think of Randy Travis's classic "Deeper Than the Holler."

These songs express a love that goes to great lengths and reaches great heights. The songs are popular because we want to experience a love like that. We want to give that kind of love; maybe more, we want to receive that kind of love. The desire is a hint that we are made for an inexhaustible love, the kind that no person can fully supply and only God can truly give. It is better than a pure romantic love—more solid, more everlasting.

Romans 8 describes a love of the strongest kind. Verses 37-39 climax Paul's exposition of God's work, accomplished for us in Christ Jesus. In Jesus, Paul tells us, God's love has triumphed and nothing can stop it. Furthermore, that love has been poured into us, so we are now "more than conquerors." Once we have received God's love, we're designed to pour that love back out to others, working for justice and peace, giving generously and with compassion.

Once we come to know the God who has gone to such lengths in reconciling us to himself, we cannot help ceaselessly beholding the mystery (1 Peter 1:10-12). Doing so increases our love for God. As our love increases, so too does our desire to live according to God's purposes. God's grace is the fuel for saints as they go about godly living. Consider God's love, draw from the well, and live the life.

Father, help me to realize the depths of your great love for me. May my response be greater love. Amen.

Session Two

Experiencing the Love of God

6. SING THE SONGS

Sing to the LORD a new song;
   sing to the LORD, all the earth. . . .
For great is the Lord and most worthy of praise.

Psalm 96:1, 4*a*

In the past three years, unexpectedly, I have become a fan of professional soccer. Our local team, Sporting Kansas City, has emerged as one of the best teams in Major League Soccer. The team plays an exciting style of soccer, always on the attack, and the players are accessible. The stadium environment is electric, and game day is always fun.

I played soccer growing up but was much more passionate about football, basketball, and baseball. In my adult years, what drew me to soccer? How did I move from apathy to fandom? Though there are many factors at play, I credit the songs.

My first experience at a Sporting match came in the Members' Stand. These are the cheapest seats in the stadium and are filled with the most passionate fans. For the duration of every match, all the fans in that section are on their feet, singing anthems and cheering the team on to success. A small group of dedicated supporters leads the section in song and other demonstrations of loyalty. Their enthusiasm is contagious. Through these fans, I experienced the love of Sporting, and I was hooked.

In most worship gatherings, singing is a major component. Those present not only listen to Scripture, engage in prayer, or hear a sermon, they lift their voices, doing their very best to make a pleasant sound, to release something from their inmost being that is a reflection of joy and gladness and longing. Often, those who know and love God most deeply do not restrict their singing to church meetings. They sing melodies while cleaning their homes, walking along quiet paths, or pausing for devotion. After an encounter with God and others who love him, these people are hooked.

Singing is a way to experience and express God's love. The songs we sing in worship remind us of God's character, God's actions on our behalf, and God's promised faithfulness in our future. They teach and equip us to grow in love for God. As the psalmist writes, "Sing to the Lord, all the earth." Join in.

Faithful, gracious, and loving God, bring to my remembrance songs that make my heart glad, that I might experience your goodness and see you as most worthy of praise. Amen.

7. A NEW FAMILY

See what great love the Father has lavished on us, that we should be called children of God! And that is what we are!

1 John 3:1*a*

One of my friends was adopted. I remember hearing him talk about it, reflecting on the fact that his biological parents turned him over to an adoption agency. He couldn't help wondering: How did that experience shape his self-understanding? Why were his parents unable to care for him? Was he unwanted or undesirable? Was he considered a mistake? What did it mean that he was not born to a family who could provide a loving, joyful home? These questions, and more, weighed on his mind.

Thankfully, my friend was adopted into a loving home. Furthermore, his adoptive parents were Christians. Through them, he was able to see that we are all orphans of sorts, seeking our heart's true home, and that in Christ we have been made part of a new family. Where earthly parents fail us, our heavenly Father lavishes us with his love. Those who come from disjointed families find that in Christ, all of us have a new family that, for all its faults, is being redeemed. Together, we experience God's love and are called to do God's will.

The nature of family, redefined in Christ, helped my friend to see that in the grand quilt of his life, his adoption was but one square. That square is part of who he is but doesn't define his worth and value as a human being. He has been included in a greater story, has been made part of an everlasting and eternal family, and is being used for God's redemptive purposes in the world.

When my friend realized this, his love for God overflowed. He was of course grateful for his earthly, adoptive family. But the notion God that had secured his adoption in Christ, claiming him as one of God's children, blew his mind and invigorated his heart with divine energy. Like John, he exclaimed, "In Christ, I am a child of God! Yes! That is what I am!"

That is what you are too. Discover God's love. Respond with an embrace.

Father, may I experience the depths of your love. In Jesus, you have claimed me as your child, brought me into your family, and given me new life. Fill me with deep joy and gladness, realizing the security I have in you. Amen.

8. THE PATTERN FOR PRAYER

Pray like this:
    Our Father who is in heaven,
        uphold the holiness of your name.
    Bring in your kingdom
        so that your will is done on earth
        as it's done in heaven.
    Give us the bread we need for today.
    Forgive us for the ways
        we have wronged you,
        just as we also forgive those
        who have wronged us.
    And don't lead us into temptation,
        but rescue us from the evil one.

Matthew 6:9-13 CEB

If I want to grow in my relationship with another person, I invite the person to coffee. We sit down and have a conversation. We begin with very basic questions, such as family of origin and work experiences, musical tastes and cinematic preferences. As time passes, the relationship grows and develops. We revisit old themes and explore new avenues. We might share burdens or learn from each other.

These conversations often take a similar shape. There is a pattern. There are formalities such as "How are you doing?" and questions about specific events, either ongoing or from the past. The familiar shape or pattern of the conversation helps the relationship to grow.

Prayer is like that. Prayer can have a pattern, and patterns help us grow in love for God. Sometimes we don't know what to pray, so Jesus guides us with what has come to be known as the Lord's Prayer, quoted above.

This simple prayer teaches us so much about who God is and the nature of our relationship with God. Jesus instructs us to address God personally, as Father, and to ask that God's name be honored, his kingdom be received, and his will be done, on earth as it is in heaven. Jesus tells us to ask the Father to provide for our basic needs, to keep us from temptation, and to preserve us from any bad thing.

This prayer helps us to sustain a conversation with God over time, providing us with simple guidelines for our relationship with God. It gives us a vision for the future and nourishment along the way. It reveals ways in which our lives are lacking and creates space where we can see God at work.

Think on these things, and pray this prayer. Through it, experience God's love and the art of conversation with God.

In closing today, read today's Scripture as it was intended for us— as training in prayer. Carefully focus on each word.

9. HOW LONG?

*How long, L*ORD*? Will you forget me forever?*
  How long will you hide your face from me?
How long must I wrestle with my thoughts
  and day after day have sorrow in my heart?
  How long will my enemy triumph over me?
*Look on me and answer, L*ORD *my God.*
  Give light to my eyes, or I will sleep in death,
and my enemy will say, "I have overcome him,"
  and my foes will rejoice when I fall.
But I trust in your unfailing love;
  my heart rejoices in your salvation.
*I will sing the L*ORD*'s praise,*
  for he has been good to me.

Psalm 13:1-6

"How long, Lord?" If you have ever stood in an airport security line, you have prayed this prayer.

You also have prayed this prayer in more serious times. You may have asked, "Where are you, God?" and received no answer. You may have wondered if God was there at all.

Life brings hardship and struggle. No exceptions are made for friends of God. Like the psalmist, we imagine during these moments that God has hidden his face and removed his presence from us.

Unlike the psalmist, however, we often are slow to claim the unfailing love of God. The psalmist trusts that God ultimately acts for the good, but we are not always sure. Scripture teaches us that we can remain confident in God's steadfast love, despite horrendous circumstances. We have not been abandoned. The psalmist declares the depth of his angst. Following his plea for help, he rests in the faithfulness of God. Praying the Psalms trains us to relate to God as the psalmist does, retaining hope in adversity.

Theologian Stanley Hauerwas has written, "We pray the Psalms not because they give expression to our religious experience—though they sometimes may do that—but because our lives are given form by praying the Psalms."[9] If you are a farmer, your life is shaped by the rhythms of the seasons, by reaping and sowing, by bountiful harvests and lean years. If you are a Christian, the Psalms likewise shape your character.

Pray these prayers. Let them get down deep. The posture of the psalmist teaches us much concerning how we can keep our faith in difficult times.

Lord, give me confidence that you are always out for my good. Like the psalmist, I know you hear my cries. Like the psalmist, I know you will remain true to your covenant. Until I experience deliverance, I wait for you. Amen.

10. THE HABIT OF PRAISE

Praise the LORD.

Praise God in his sanctuary;
*   praise him in his mighty heavens.*
Praise him for his acts of power;
*   praise him for his surpassing greatness.*
Praise him with the sounding of the trumpet,
*   praise him with the harp and lyre,*
praise him with timbrel and dancing,
*   praise him with the strings and pipe,*
praise him with the clash of cymbals,
*   praise him with resounding cymbals.*
Let everything that has breath praise the LORD.

Praise the LORD.

Psalm 150

One of my close friends went to a large state college. There, on the evening prior to each football game, a horde of students gather to practice the traditional cheers and yells they will thunder the following day. In this way, the students ignite their enthusiasm and display their support for the team. The next day, they show their love for the team and do their best to spur it on to victory. This tradition instills in the students not only a love for their football program but also a love for their university.

We learn to love God in a like manner. Gathering with other Christians in worship ingrains the habit of praise through song and sermon and prayer. Praise is our right response to the love of God. Praise results from a clear vision of God's character. As we see God's acts of power and surpassing greatness, we take whatever we have and turn it into an instrument of praise. It might be a harp or timbrel or lyre. It might be our voice or our hands and feet.

We might praise while gathered with the saints as the church. Or we might continue our praise and worship of God as we care for friends or family, or serve neighbors through our work. Every time we draw a breath, we remember that praise is right. We pray, earnestly, that everything else that draws breath will praise the Lord.

Praise is a habit, and it is pervasive. As we experience the love of God, every other venture is injected with a newfound, redemptive energy. We're part of a larger story, a larger work. We have a role to play.

Are you playing your part?

Praise the Lord.

God, who is worthy of all praise, teach me to worship with all that I am and all that I have. Help me to see that praising you is a right response to the vastness of your love. Amen.

The Transforming Love of God

11. BEARING FRUIT

But the fruit of the Spirit is love, joy, peace, forbearance, kindness, goodness, faithfulness, gentleness and self-control. Against such things there is no law.

Galatians 5:22-23

If you go to an apple orchard and fruit is in season, you expect to pick apples. If you go to a vineyard, you expect grapes. An orange grove produces oranges.

And the Spirit of God produces love, joy, peace, forbearance, kindness, goodness, faithfulness, gentleness, and self-control. That is the Spirit's work.

The love of God has transforming power. It can profoundly change you, causing you to display those virtues. Faith in Jesus brings the gift of the Holy Spirit, who empowers all who believe. The Bible gives us a vision for how we should lead our lives, but the Spirit provides the power to do it. Discipleship to Christ should lead you to "walk by the Spirit," not by the flesh (Galatians 5:16). Through an increasing reliance on the Spirit's work, in Christ, you become a new creature (2 Corinthians 5:17).

In the deepest and truest sense, when our lives are transformed, it is an act of God's grace. Today's Scripture reading is not *prescriptive* (do this; be well), but *descriptive* (this is the life the Spirit brings). How, then, do we obtain such a life? The answer is found in discipleship to Jesus.

Learning to do everything Jesus did and said is itself an experience of the transformative power of God's love. Jesus leads by example, offering to be with us as we walk through life (Matthew 28:18-20). As we read the Gospels, we watch Jesus retreating to lonely places to pray. We see that he knows and therefore must have studied Scripture. We find Jesus serving others, welcoming the outcast, seeking out the lost, and proclaiming good news to captives (Luke 4:18-19). We also see him embodying love, joy, peace, forbearance, kindness, goodness, faithfulness, gentleness, and self-control—the "fruit of the Spirit." We must learn from him.

If you wish to be a person who bears such fruit, ask Jesus to teach you. Surround yourself with others learning his ways, those schooled in Jesus' life. The best teachers might not be those you would expect. But here's a hint: "By their fruit you will recognize them" (Matthew 7:16).

Holy Spirit, change my life and transform me by the power of your love. Amen.

12. CAVING

So then, if anyone is in Christ, that person is part of the new creation. The old things have gone away, and look, new things have arrived!

2 Corinthians 5:17 CEB

·

My wife, Molly, is a pastor. Of the many hats pastors wear, one is that of caver. Caving is the hobby or practice of exploring caves. Whether by choice, accidental admission, or sideways invitation, Molly is called by the desperate to the dark, treacherous depths of their lives. She is asked to rappel into the brokenness, sift through wreckage, and shed light on the soul, revealing what truly is there. She descends with those she pastors, takes their hands, and leads the way out of the pit.

My wife learned this pattern from Jesus.

In the Book of Philippians, Paul writes that Jesus, "being in very nature God, did not consider equality with God something to be used to his own advantage; rather, he made himself nothing . . . being made in human likeness . . . he humbled himself by becoming obedient to death—even death on a cross!" (2:6-8). In Ephesians, Paul declares that Christ's ascent to heaven raises the question: "What does 'he ascended' mean except that he also descended to the lower, earthly regions?" (4:9). A thread runs through the New Testament: God in the flesh, Jesus, descended from heaven to lead us as one who serves. He leads us in his way, imparting new life to us. The life that was in him is given to us—the gift of eternal life.

I don't know your story. But I'm sure there is some dark corner of your life, some part of you that isn't quite right, an emptiness or brokenness, some desperation you've quietly suppressed. You've pursued money or power or sex. Those gods have failed you. You're angry; you don't know why. Pick your vice. Name your tragedy. Hope seems lost.

But Christ came to redeem you. Christ came to make you new. Christ came to rid you of those old, false idols, to reorient your heart toward the good, true, and beautiful—things ultimately found in Christ himself. Christ descended to our world, and he will descend into the muck and mire of your mess, shedding light, offering a hand, and leading the way.

There is hope, transformation, new creation.

The old has gone. The new has come.

Jesus, you came to make me new. Increase my faith. Transform me, inside out, for your glory. In your name. Amen.

13. "I WAS"

So, my brothers and sisters, you also died to the law through the body of Christ, that you might belong to another, to him who was raised from the dead, in order that we might bear fruit for God. For when we were in the realm of the flesh, the sinful passions aroused by the law were at work in us, so that we bore fruit for death. But now, by dying to what once bound us, we have been released from the law so that we serve in the new way of the Spirit, and not in the old way of the written code.

Romans 7:4-6

My friend Scott McClellan is a great storyteller. He is passionate about helping others live a good story, specifically God's story. He serves as communications pastor at Irving Bible Church in Texas.

In his book *Tell Me a Story*, Scott writes, "The power of narrative starts with the beauty of the words, 'I was.'"[10] All of us have a past. It could be that you have been a victim. It could be that you have been the victimizer. As we tell the story, the critical moment is when a change takes place, moving us from one way of being to another. Pivot points help the story take shape. Saying "I was" indicates a turn, one that is critical to living a powerful story.

In Romans, Paul tells a good story, one we want to live. Paul's good story is the sweeping narrative of God's salvation, brought to a climax in the person and work of Jesus. Paul says that in Christ, a death has taken place, and now there is new life, transformation. In our reading today, Paul says those "bound" by the law and living "in the realm of the flesh" have now been "released" to "serve in the new way of the Spirit."

What does this mean? God has accomplished our salvation in Jesus Christ, who now takes up residence at the center of our lives. The Spirit then empowers us to do the things God desires for us to do.

Today, walk by the Spirit. See that in Christ you can say, "I was." Walk in newness of life.

Spirit of God, get down to the level of my motivations, and set them right. Help me to do things according to your way, freed for obedience to you. Amen.

14. A NEW WAY OF SEEING

Don't be conformed to the patterns of this world, but be transformed by the renewing of your minds so that you can figure out what God's will is—what is good and pleasing and mature.

Romans 12:2 CEB

In May 1961, John Lewis and other civil rights activists boarded a Greyhound bus headed for Montgomery, Alabama. When they arrived, these "Freedom Riders" were beaten by an angry mob opposed to integration. On that day, the Montgomery Police Department failed to protect these citizens from violence.

More than fifty years later, Georgia Congressman John Lewis returned to Montgomery for a civil rights event and, to his surprise, received an apology from the city's police chief, Kevin Murphy.[11] Murphy went so far as to admit that the Montgomery Police Department of that era had wrongly enforced unjust laws. Lewis was deeply moved. The two stood united, hopeful for a better future.

There had been a transformation.

Christians are called to a kind of transformation, a new way of seeing, a renewal of our thinking patterns. The Montgomery police force in 1961 had a way of thinking and seeing that they assumed was right. But Martin Luther King Jr. and a group of committed leaders had another way of seeing, another way of thinking, which I believe was more deeply faithful to the vision found in Scripture. Under the guidance of the Holy Spirit, we learn from Scripture what it means to think and act according to God's will. While the work of transformation is God's, Scripture is an indispensable resource for the renewing of our minds. If you wish to grow in the knowledge of what is "good and pleasing and mature" as one of God's children, study the Bible.

In the Bible you will find numerous examples of faithfulness to God—people who are worth following. You will also find numerous examples of unfaithfulness, and in these you will uncover many pitfalls to avoid. The Bible includes commands that show us the right way to live, and others that specifically instruct us concerning what not to do. Most important, the Bible gives us a story that transforms our story, by the power of Christ.

Let God change your way of seeing so that you come to love God—heart, soul, mind, and strength.

God, renew my mind, so that I might know and do your perfect will. In Christ's holy name I ask. Amen.

15. THE TREE AND THE FRUIT

By their fruit you will recognize them. Do people pick grapes from thornbushes, or figs from thistles? Likewise, every good tree bears good fruit, but a bad tree bears bad fruit. A good tree cannot bear bad fruit, and a bad tree cannot bear good fruit. Every tree that does not bear good fruit is cut down and thrown into the fire. Thus, by their fruit you will recognize them.

Matthew 7:16-20

During my youth, our family took a number of long road trips. Portable gaming devices, iPods, and laptop computers had not yet been introduced, so I opted to listen to the radio and look out the window. There was much to see.

As we drove down the Texas highways, we passed a number of farms. I learned to distinguish a cornfield from a cotton patch and a dairy cow from a longhorn steer. I didn't always know the difference right away; I would have to ask. But I had guides who helped me sort one kind of crop, or livestock, from another.

Jesus often spoke to common folks, many of whom had an agricultural background. Grape vines and fig trees—those are things Jesus' hearers knew. They could tell one from the other; they knew what each produced. They also knew that a healthy tree was a good tree. These trees were valued and were expected to bring forth plenty for harvest. Bad or unproductive trees were a different story.

In Matthew 7, Jesus uses the example of the good and bad tree as a lesson concerning whom to follow. He explains that if you look at what is produced in the lives of certain teachers and religious leaders, you can be pretty certain which to follow and which to avoid. However, Jesus' standard of judgment raises another question: "What kind of tree am I?"

That question concerns character and heart. Who am I at the core? Does my life bring forth good or bad fruit? Do I need to be transformed, so my life will display fruit that is pleasing to God? At some level, the answer should be yes.

Thankfully, that is the business God is in: remaking us from the inside out.

Jesus, I want to be a good tree, producing good fruit for you. Transform me by the power of your love. In your name. Amen.

Choosing to Trust God's Love

16. CONFIDENCE IN GOD

Going a little farther, he fell with his face to the ground and prayed, "My Father, if it is possible, may this cup be taken from me. Yet not as I will, but as you will."

Matthew 26:39

There is a hymn that goes "Whatever my lot, Thou hast taught me to say, / It is well, it is well, with my soul."[12] Those beautiful words have been a source of comfort for many passing through strife.

The man who wrote "It Is Well with My Soul" was named Horatio G. Spafford.[13] Spafford lived in the latter half of the nineteenth century, was married, was a successful lawyer, and had five children. He was a faithful Christian.

In 1870, Spafford faced the first of many trials. His son, Horatio Jr., contracted scarlet fever and died. In 1871, the Great Chicago Fire consumed many of his real estate investments, and he lost most of his fortune. In 1873, Spafford's wife, Anna, and their four daughters set sail across the Atlantic on vacation, with Horatio planning to join them later. But their vessel, the *Ville du Havre*, was struck by another ship and sank. Anna survived, but their daughters were lost.

After receiving a telegram from Anna about their loss, Horatio set out to bring his wife home. While passing near the spot where his children had died, the captain of the vessel informed Horatio, who returned to his cabin and wrote the words we sing in this famous hymn.

Horatio Spafford trusted in God's love despite immense suffering. He never understood why he underwent such ordeals, but his confidence in God did not waver. Perhaps he remembered the experience of Jesus, who likewise underwent immense suffering. Yet Christ's suffering was not in vain. Through it, God brought about redemption and new life.

When we suffer, we too can have confidence in God's good purposes. We can trust in God's love. We may never come to understand why we are allowed to endure great hardship. But we can trust that whatever may come, God will work all things together for the good (Romans 8:28).

Lord, help me to trust in your love, in good times and in bad. Give me an unwavering hope that you will work all things to the good. Amen.

17. AN EXPERIENCED GUIDE

Trust in the L<small>ORD</small> with all your heart
and lean not on your own understanding;
in all your ways submit to him,
and he will make your paths straight.

Proverbs 3:5-6

A few years ago, my in-laws urged my wife, Molly, and me to become certified scuba divers. After watching instructional videos, completing book work, and working with an instructor in a swimming pool, we finished our training on a family trip. I'm not always adventuresome, but scuba diving has become one of my favorite hobbies.

After a few dives, we had an opportunity to explore a reef at night. Night diving is different. You have to bring your own flashlight, the creatures are unique, and there is a heightened level of danger. On the descent, you are shrouded in darkness until your guide discerns that the group is at the appropriate depth and turns on his light. As you fall through the water in the darkness, it can be scary.

Being with an experienced guide, however, meant we were in good hands. During the darkest moments we may have been anxious, but ultimately we were confident. When we turned the lights back on and explored the reef's features, beholding the living things under the water, we saw that our guide had brought us to a good and beautiful place. Our initial trust was validated through experience.

In Proverbs we read, "Trust in the LORD with all your heart and lean not on your own understanding." When we trust in God, there may be times when we don't see clearly, and it feels as though we are surrounded by darkness. Most Christians can tell stories of such times. I certainly can.

But after a time, the light comes on, and it is clear we have never been alone. God has been there all along, guiding and directing us, seeing to it that our paths have been straighter than we've supposed. God brings us out of darkness and takes us to a good and beautiful place, affirming us as his children and showing us his ways.

The journey begins and continues with an abiding faith in a God who is good. Trust his love, and rejoice in him.

God, you are my guide in light and darkness, leading me forward in a way that is good. Increase my trust in your great love. Amen.

18. A COUNTERINTUITIVE LIFE

Bless your enemies; no cursing under your breath. Laugh with your happy friends when they're happy; share tears when they're down. Get along with each other; don't be stuck-up. Make friends with nobodies; don't be the great somebody.

Romans 12:14-16 *The Message*

Trusting God's love leads to a counterintuitive life. So much of our life training is turned upside down; so many of our usual patterns are disrupted. I'd like to think, for example, that I don't have any enemies. But there are people around me who vote differently from me, think differently from me, and advocate for causes I oppose. Jesus himself taught "Love your enemies" (Matthew 5:44), but I have to admit that sometimes I don't want to.

"Laugh with your happy friends" appears easier, until I remember that my friends are happy because they are celebrating a pregnancy, and my wife and I just suffered a miscarriage. Then I become bitter. And I don't always want to get along. If I'm honest, there are days when I want to be at war, and I'm willing to crush anyone who gets in my way. I am violent. Trusting God's love isn't easy, because God loves his enemies, and that's not just pious talk. Jesus Christ died for his enemies, for people who opposed him.

God is the true source of joy. Where there is laughter, God is in the center of it. When people mourn, God comforts them (Isaiah 61:2-3). His greatness is in his lowliness. God is the great somebody because he was willing to become a nobody—born of a poor virgin in a backwater town called Bethlehem. We struggle to trust God's love, because it makes our lives seem so hollow by contrast, so void of goodness and beauty and truth.

But that's where the gospel comes in. We have been redeemed. The life that was in Jesus is the same life Jesus wants to put in us. We don't simply strive to be like Jesus, though he is our example. We put ourselves in his hands and ask him to remake us. He does. When you face a challenge today, trust in him.

Jesus, do in me what I am unable to do by my own power. Help me trust your love. Amen.

19. A HOUSE FIT FOR A KING

And whoever does not carry their cross and follow me cannot be my disciple.

Luke 14:27

Trusting God's love means taking up a cross and following Jesus. The cross is appropriate, for there are things about you that will have to go, that need to be put to death. You'll have to be remade. Jesus did not come to make us nice, but to make us new.

C. S. Lewis described it well. He said to imagine yourself as a living house. God shows up and begins to rebuild. Things go well at first. God fixes drains and plugs leaks, things you knew were wrong and which you expected God to address.

But soon thereafter, God begins knocking out walls "in a way that hurts abominably and does not seem to make sense. You ask, 'What on earth is he up to?' The explanation is that he is building quite a different house from the one you thought of—throwing out a new wing here, putting on an extra floor there, running up towers, making courtyards."

Lewis concludes, "You thought you were going to be made into a decent little cottage: but he is building up a palace. He intends to come and live in it himself."[14]

Too often, we think becoming Christians will result in being just a slightly nicer version of ourselves. We believe a dash of religion will make us a little more appealing and acceptable to God. Thankfully, God loves us too much to let us retain our delusions.

In what areas of your life do you need to trust God's love and be made new? You may struggle with anger, lust, or pride. You may be a glutton or a gossip or a cheat. Ask God, the master craftsman, to pinpoint your problems and repair the rot. Learn from him the way of the cross, putting to death wrongful desires and false motives. Let him put something better in its place.

Trust God's love for the renovation of your heart and the renewal of your life. It might not always be easy and smooth. But the result will be good—a house fit for a King.

Jesus, I wish to be your disciple. I'm ready to take up my cross. Put to death everything in me that hinders you, and give life to all in me that brings you glory. Amen.

20. PLAN A FAST

Then Jesus was led by the Spirit into the wilderness to be tempted by the devil. After fasting forty days and forty nights, he was hungry. The tempter came to him and said, "If you are the Son of God, tell these stones to become bread."
Jesus answered, "It is written: 'Man shall not live on bread alone, but on every word that comes from the mouth of God.'"

Matthew 4:1-4

There are many ways we can learn to trust God's goodness and love, but fasting has proven itself over time as one of the great disciplines of our faith. Through fasting, we disengage from our normal life patterns and engage God for the provision of our sustenance. As we purposefully and literally create empty spaces within ourselves, we invite God to fill those spaces with love, goodness, and grace, so we might further come to trust him.

When most of us consider fasting, we think of abstention from eating, and this certainly can prove beneficial. When we fast from our meals, we experience solidarity with the poor—there are still many who, on a daily basis, struggle to secure daily meals. We can put aside the money we would have spent at a restaurant, and give it away. We also experience solidarity with Jesus in his wilderness experience, and we learn what it can mean to be fed and nourished by the power of God (Matthew 4:4; John 4:32-34).

Abstention from eating is one form of fasting. But in modern times, we have other options available to us. Fasting from media is one of my most important Christian practices. We can fast from the daily news or from our phones. We can turn off the radio or take long breaks from our social media networks. We might not be gluttons for food, but we may be for information.

Once we turn down the noise, what will we hear? Suddenly, God's leading and direction might become clearer.

Plan a fast. Mark it on your calendar. Tell friends in your learning community, and ask them to hold you accountable. Following your fast, plan a time to sit down with your friends and discuss the experience.

God, you provide for my every need. I ask that in fasting, you would speak to me. Show me how to trust you, as Jesus trusted you in the wilderness. Amen.

Session Five

The Love of God in the Sacraments

21. THE MEAL

For I received from the Lord what I also passed on to you: The Lord Jesus, on the night he was betrayed, took bread, and when he had given thanks, he broke it and said, "This is my body, which is for you; do this in remembrance of me." In the same way, after supper he took the cup, saying, "This cup is the new covenant in my blood; do this, whenever you drink it, in remembrance of me."
1 Corinthians 11:23-25

Every year at Christmas, my family gathers and shares a meal. Everyone brings a different dish. My aunt Jamie prepares buttery rolls. My mom prepares sweet potatoes loaded with brown sugar

117

and marshmallows. My grandfather prepares beef tenderloin cooked to perfection. It is some of the finest food I eat all year.

Following the meal, we gather in the living room and sing, then share the highlight of our year. We receive a gift. These traditions bind us, solidifying certain dimensions of our character. There is a real, felt experience of love at these gatherings.

When I think back over the course of my life, I remember other important meals. I'm sure you do too. When Jesus gave us a meal by which to remember him, he powerfully leveraged the act of eating together to create something new. Jesus retold the story of his people, Israel. By extension, he retold the story of the world.

When we celebrate the Lord's meal, we signify that everyone is invited to God's table; everyone is welcome. We announce that in the body and blood of Christ, peace with God and neighbor has been made possible. Love has been poured out in the body and blood of Jesus. As we give thanks, take, eat, and drink, that same love is abundantly poured out on us, the church, the body of Christ.

Next time you celebrate the Lord's meal, look carefully at those present, whom God so loved. As you leave, look carefully at those on the streets, in your neighborhood, in your workplace, whom God so loved and who, like us, are invited to God's table. For them, may you be the body of Christ.

Father, help me to love you through the meal we celebrate in the name of the Son. I ask you to do these things by the power of the Holy Spirit. Amen.

22. THE TRUTH ABOUT OURSELVES

And so John the Baptist appeared in the wilderness, preaching a baptism of repentance for the forgiveness of sins. The whole Judean countryside and all the people of Jerusalem went out to him. Confessing their sins, they were baptized by him in the Jordan River.

Mark 1:4-5

In 2009 I visited Israel. One of our stops was at the Jordan River. Many on the trip entered the waters for baptism, or for a ceremony of remembering baptism. In some small way, they wanted to identify with Jesus and John the Baptist. They desired to repent of sin, receive assurance of forgiveness, and express a renewed commitment to discipleship. Many found this experience very powerful.

Baptism is powerful for many reasons. It is symbolic of new life, an outward sign of an inward reality. As I looked upon the faces of those being baptized, there was joy and gladness and hope. Through baptism, these people experienced the love of God.

In Mark's Gospel, we are told that many people came out to the wilderness to be baptized by John. John's baptism was one "of repentance for the forgiveness of sins." Those who visited John "came confessing their sins." These people told the truth and were cleansed.

It might unsettle us to think about it, but one of the ways we receive love is through telling the truth about ourselves. This is risky. Instead of a facade, we each show our true face. Love comes when we find we are welcomed anyway.

Baptism shows we are accepted by God—not arbitrarily, as though God were simply a nice person, willing to overlook our faults; but in a profound way, secured by the death of Jesus on the cross, who paid for the sins we confess. In baptism, we know that God has taken our filth upon himself, washing us clean. When we confess to God the truth about ourselves, we can remember that before even one of those sins was committed, Jesus died to save us.

God shows us love through baptism. If you have not yet been baptized, what are you waiting for? If you have, remember your baptism, and be assured of God's love.

God, my sins have been forgiven, by the grace of Jesus Christ. May I encounter your love in baptism, where you remind us we are accepted and our sins are forgiven. Amen.

23. AFTER INITIATION

Then Jesus came to them and said, "All authority in heaven and on earth has been given to me. Therefore go and make disciples of all nations, baptizing them in the name of the Father and of the Son and of the Holy Spirit, and teaching them to obey everything I have commanded you. And surely I am with you always, to the very end of the age."

Matthew 28:18-20

During my sophomore year of college I joined an organization committed to serving my school. Our mission was to promote an active interest in the athletic, academic, traditional, and cultural aspects of university life. We coordinated campus events and cared for the mascots. There was always work to do.

As with other college student organizations, there was a recruitment process, when members got to know prospects and prospects learned about the organization. But once a prospect was selected, there was an initiation process. We received pins to wear on our shirts and were asked to dress a certain way on campus. We had meetings to attend and tasks to accomplish. New patterns signaled to everyone in our circle that our lives had changed. Following initiation, a public transformation took place.

Baptism is similar. In it, we engage in a public act that sets us apart as members of a new body, the body of Christ. Jesus commanded his followers to baptize new disciples as a means of initiation. Baptism is a sign of affiliation and commitment. It is God's gift to us.

When we are taken beneath the waters, we signal our intent to continue in Christian discipleship and learn everything Jesus did and taught. Moreover, we signal that in Christ, we have been chosen to become part of his people, the church. Our response to God in baptism is preceded by God's love toward us (1 John 4:19).

Whether you received baptism as an infant or an adult, God, by grace, has welcomed you as part of his family. Reflect on your baptism and the moments that followed, identifying formative moments for your growth as a Christian disciple. If you have not been baptized, talk to a pastor. Consider making your association with Jesus public, plain for all to see.

Jesus, in baptism you affirm that I have been received as your disciple. Train me according to your ways; form me in your love. Amen.

24. BEAUTY IN SIMPLICITY, RICHNESS IN COMPLEXITY

*On the first day of the week we came together to break bread.
Paul spoke to the people and, because he intended to leave the
next day, kept on talking until midnight.*

Acts 20:7

Growing up, I was part of a church that observed the Lord's Supper once a quarter. For a couple of years in Kansas City, I was part of a church that celebrated the meal every week. Now, I'm part of a church that serves Holy Communion in worship once every month.

Different churches celebrate the Lord's meal in different ways and at different times. Why is this?

Today's Scripture states, "On the first day of the week we came together to break bread." The earliest Christians celebrated Jesus' meal. As often as they did, they remembered him and were recharged for mission in the world. They thanked God for what the elements signified—Jesus' death on the cross and the forgiveness of sins he secured on the world's behalf. Breaking bread was vital for their lives as Christians.

How often do you celebrate Jesus' meal? What does your church teach concerning the Eucharist, and why? Denominations vary in their teaching. As a devotional exercise, you might wish to spend a little time researching your tradition's doctrine. Deeper knowledge of Communion will lead to a more robust experience as you watch the liturgy unfold and participate in it.

I can't claim to know all the reasons why churches differ in their practice of the Lord's Supper. But I do know that Communion was a regular part of the earliest apostles' lives, and participation in the meal has long been regarded as a mark of the church. It's important. N. T. Wright states that in the meal, "symbols of the natural world become vehicles of the heavenly world, of which we are called to be citizens."[15] Beauty is found in the simplicity of the act, and richness is found in the complexity of its meaning. Jesus chose common symbols—the bread and cup—to call us forth to life in his kingdom, to remind us of his grace, and to reenergize us for mission.

As it has been written, "Taste and see that the LORD is good" (Psalm 34:8).

Holy Spirit, lead me to deeper knowledge of Holy Communion, that I may grow as Jesus' disciple. Amen.

25. A NEW STORY

Or don't you know that all of us who were baptized into Christ Jesus were baptized into his death? We were therefore buried with him through baptism into death in order that, just as Christ was raised from the dead through the glory of the Father, we too may live a new life.

Romans 6:3-4

When I was a young boy, I was baptized at a Sunday evening church service. My pastor guided me in saying these words: "I take God as my Father, Jesus as my Savior, and the Holy Spirit as my guide. This I do freely, completely, and forever." He then laid me under the water and said, "Buried with Christ in baptism, and risen to walk in newness of life." I burst forth from the water, and something had changed.

What had changed, however, was not so clear. That would take years to discover, and I'm still figuring it all out. As Paul writes, in baptism we are joined to Christ in his death, so that "just as Christ was raised from the dead through the glory of the Father," we might experience a new life—a resurrection life—that is like his. After baptism, everything about us has new significance.

Theologian Stanley Hauerwas rightly claims, "Through baptism we do not simply learn the story, but we become part of that story."[16] Having been baptized, my life is no longer what it was. I've been made part of a larger narrative, the story of God's redemption of the world. I might be a bit player. I might have scenes where God brings me to center stage. But in baptism, my life is no longer aimless. I have an important role to play in an unfolding cosmic drama. I want to play my part well.

Playing my part well requires discipleship, learning from Jesus and from the church about the Christian story. Through discipleship I'll learn to pray for my persecutors and love my enemies. I'll learn to bear the burdens of others. I'll learn to be generous, to have joy, and to achieve even greater things. In baptism, I'll experience God's love by being made part of a good story. And through it all, God will be glorified.

Lord Jesus, in my baptism I have been made part of your story. Thank you. Teach me to play my part well. Amen.

Session Six

The Love of God as the Mark of the Church

26. "MAY WE NOT LOVE ALIKE?"

I in them and you in me—so that they may be brought to complete unity. Then the world will know that you sent me and have loved them even as you have loved me.

John 17:23

In the aftermath of Hurricane Katrina, a group from my church traveled to the small community of Dulac, Louisiana. We stayed at a mission station of the United Methodist Committee on Relief and received our marching orders. With other United Methodist Christians, we worked to rebuild the homes of the people affected by the hurricane and help them piece their lives back together.

Within Methodism, and within other Christian denominations, there is theological diversity, difference of worship styles, and a variety of missional emphases. But when there is work to be done, there is unity, found in Jesus. Much of the work done in Dulac was excellent. Our mission was to meet physical needs, but also to listen, inviting those we served to tell their stories, mourn their losses, and move forward. In word and deed, we did our very best to demonstrate the love of Jesus.

In John 17, Jesus asked his Father to foster unity among the disciples. He asked it for those closest to him and those far off. Jesus knew that when his followers were united, the world would see the power of God's love.

John Wesley, in his sermon "Catholic Spirit," famously argued for Christian unity. Wesley wrote, "Though we cannot think alike, may we not love alike? May we not be of one heart, though we are not of one opinion? Without all doubt, we may. Herein all the children of God may unite, notwithstanding these smaller differences. These remaining as they are, they may forward one another in love and in good works."[17] Wesley didn't trivialize theological differences; instead, he sought to establish a basis for partnership rooted in the love of God.

How can you work with other Christians in your fellowship, demonstrating the love of God? Further, how can you work with Christians outside your immediate circle, in an effort to give a common witness to Jesus?

Christian unity demonstrates to the world the love of God. Work for it.

God Almighty, may I foster unity, not division. May I build bridges, not burn them. May I extend my hand to other Christians, not turn my back. By this, may others see your love. Amen.

27. CALLED OUT

I tell you that you are Peter. And I'll build my church on this rock.
The gates of the underworld won't be able to stand against it.

Matthew 16:18 CEB

Most of us like to think that our spiritual lives are individualistic pursuits. "I come to the garden, alone," we sing. "Just me and Jesus," we imagine. "Spiritual, but not religious," we intone, which often is another way of saying we can chart our own path. I'm guilty of this. But God never intended it that way. Loved as individuals, we are made part of a collective. We don't have to make it up as we go; the saints have gone before us. Thank God.

The Greek word for church, *ekklesia*, means those who have been "called out." The church is made up of the called-out people of God. To be called by Christ means you are called to his people. Christianity is social; holiness is communal. As John Wesley wrote, there is "no holiness but social holiness."[18] Jesus did not look at Peter and say, "I'll make you a great individual." No, he said he'd make Peter an indispensable part of a body, a church, a people called out together for God's purposes.

It is when we are together that the rubber hits the road. Jesus told us, "By this everyone will know that you are my disciples, if you love one another" (John 13:35 TNIV). Paul wrote, "Be completely humble and gentle; be patient" (Ephesians 4:2). James wrote, "Confess your sins to each other and pray for each other" (James 5:16). The author of Hebrews added, "Encourage one another" (Hebrews 3:13). Peter urged, "Offer hospitality to one another" (1 Peter 4:9). All of them agreed: without one another, we can't be the people God has called us to be.

Love is action, and it is known and experienced in community. Jesus said that "the gates of the underworld" would not be able to stand the advances of the church. That puts us on the offensive. When we love one another as Jesus called us to love, then God, through us, overcomes the flames of hell.

Go to hell, and bring the saints with you. Jesus leads the way. Make sure he's out front. Arm yourselves with love, demonstrated by Christ and his cross, poured out on us by the Spirit's power.

Jesus, you have joined me to the church. May I walk the way of love in fellowship with your people. Amen.

28. A FOUNDATION TO BUILD ON

As God's household, you are built on the foundation of the apostles and prophets with Christ Jesus himself as the cornerstone. The whole building is joined together in him, and it grows up into a temple that is dedicated to the Lord.

Ephesians 2:20-21 CEB

Like a lot of young boys, I played war growing up. The woods behind my house were the battlefield. My friends and I would build forts. A great deal of creativity was required to pull together enough scrap wood, old tires, twine, nails, camouflage netting, duct tape, discarded guttering, and fallen branches to provide cover from passersby. Our little army, consisting of my neighbors and me, enjoyed the process.

Though some of those structures were great, none of them lasted. Bad weather knocked them down, or our main supports gave way to rot and fell. Other people walked those woods too, and groups of older boys took pleasure in destroying what we had raised. Each time a fort was ripped down, I was disappointed.

Empires come and go, nations rise and fall, forts are built and destroyed. But the kingdom of God is everlasting. Jesus said, "Heaven and earth will pass away, but my words will never pass away" (Matthew 24:35). He added that people who build their lives on his teachings are like a wise person who builds a house on rock, so secure that the worst of storms won't wash it away (Matthew 7:24-27).

In Ephesians 2, the church is also likened to a building. The teaching of the apostles is the foundation, and Jesus himself is the cornerstone. Built on these key elements, God's temple—the church—takes on a particular shape.

As God's people, we have a foundation to build on. We love, serve, and witness in a way that aligns with Jesus and his earliest students. We read the Bible and study, very carefully, the lives of the best exemplars that have come before us. They teach us how to love God and love others.

Be careful how you build, what you build on, and whom you build with. Grow up strong and sturdy, in grace, as part of God's temple. No one will pull you down. No storm will wash you away. And forever, you will have great joy.

Lord Jesus, may I build my life on you. In your name. Amen.

29. A LOT LIKE JESUS

I needed clothes and you clothed me, I was sick and you looked after me, I was in prison and you came to visit me.'

"Then the righteous will answer him, 'Lord, when did we see you hungry and feed you, or thirsty and give you something to drink? When did we see you a stranger and invite you in, or needing clothes and clothe you? When did we see you sick or in prison and go to visit you?'

"The King will reply, 'Truly I tell you, whatever you did for one of the least of these brothers and sisters of mine, you did for me.'"

Matthew 25:36-40

In spring 2013, the Roman Catholic Church named a new pope. Jorge Mario Bergoglio, a native of Argentina, chose the name Pope Francis, identifying with Francis of Assisi, a mendicant friar and founder of the Franciscan order, and Francis Xavier, a key figure in the Jesuit tradition. At the outset of his papacy, Pope Francis began doing strange things. He refused traditional garments worn by popes of the recent past. He greeted people following worship the way a normal priest would. He asked his people to pray for him as a gesture of humility. And on the Thursday prior to his first Easter as pope, he arranged to observe the mass in a youth prison, where he would wash and kiss the feet of twelve prisoners.[19]

It's clear this pope has considered Jesus' words. He also seems to be following them.

In the parable told in today's Scripture, Jesus expects his people to clothe the naked, look after the sick, visit the imprisoned, feed the hungry, give drink to the thirsty, and welcome the stranger. When you do these things, it's as if you are doing them for Jesus. If you do these actions with great love, you bring glory to God.

We are able to do these things, not because we are particularly special, but because Jesus has redeemed us. The gospel helps us to see that, through Christ's poverty, we have been made rich and have been given all that we need to serve him, out of love.
Follow Jesus' words. In doing them, you will be blessed.

God, who reigns in heaven, give me grace that I might follow Jesus' words. Help me to see you in the poor, the stranger, the needy. Amen.

30. LIVE THE VISION

The believers devoted themselves to the apostles' teaching, to the community, to their shared meals, and to their prayers. A sense of awe came over everyone. God performed many wonders and signs through the apostles. All the believers were united and shared everything. They would sell pieces of property and possessions and distribute the proceeds to everyone who needed them. Every day, they met together in the temple and ate in their homes. They shared food with gladness and simplicity. They praised God and demonstrated God's goodness to everyone. The Lord added daily to the community those who were being saved.

Acts 2:42-47 CEB

If you have ever wondered what the church should look like, just read today's Scripture. However, when you continue reading in the Book of Acts, you'll find that the church as described here lasted about five minutes. But the story of these earliest moments was recorded for our benefit, to show us what is possible in Christ. It is all here: discipleship (learning from the apostles' teaching); fellowship (community, meeting house to house); worship (the meal, meeting in the temple courts); and service (selling possessions, sharing food, demonstrating goodness). These early Christians prayed, practiced simplicity, and were generous to those in need. People outside the church witnessed and were attracted to what was happening: "The Lord added daily to the community those who were being saved." In word and deed, the church proclaimed the good news about Jesus. Outsiders became insiders.

With a little imagination, we can see that this is possible even in today's world. The church could be like this. Sometimes it is. If you don't see it where you are, start with three or four. Learn together, eat together, serve your community, and give away your life. Ask God, in prayer, to increase your number. When challenges and hardship come, remember the early church! Then return to the vision, forgive, and ask God to work, through you, with power.

Casting a vision and seeing it realized will require your participation, maybe even your leadership. Now that you've seen what is possible, pray that it will come to be. Live for it, paying attention all the while to how and where God is at work. Wherever you see God in action, name it and give thanks.

God, the church is your vehicle for accomplishing your work. May we be faithful to the vision in Acts. Once again, may the church be so. May your kingdom come, through me. Amen.

Serving God

Session One
How and Why
We Serve God

1. ON A MISSION

Jesus went through all the towns and villages, teaching in their synagogues, proclaiming the good news of the kingdom and healing every disease and sickness.

Matthew 9:35

Sometime in the distant past, I got the idea that Christianity was only about saving souls, getting fire insurance from hell, seeing what lies beyond the grave, and opening up a path to heaven. I think that in some circles those concepts still prevail. But when I realized Christianity is more than that, I discovered new worlds and new possibilities, all of which are deeply challenging and immeasurably good.

As we read in today's Scripture, during his ministry Jesus went from town to town, describing eternity in a way we might find hard to imagine. Jesus spoke about "the good news of the kingdom," and what he announced was enacted in the here and now. He taught and we must continue to teach what the kingdom is like. But as we teach, we also proclaim God's kingdom among us by demonstrating what God's reign looks like. We heal "every disease and sickness," not only in the miraculous sense, but through health care and education and countless small, patient acts of love. Serving God in Jesus' way means more than we might previously have thought. It does not just entail inviting more people to believe in Jesus, though it certainly includes that responsibility. Serving God involves work—the work of the Kingdom.

What will that look like for you? It might mean taking a new step—participating in a church ministry to the sick and the downtrodden, such as a soup kitchen, a health clinic, or a clothing closet. It might mean activism—engaging as a Christian in public life and casting a vision that helps the entire community to thrive, as was done by Christian abolitionists William Wilberforce and John Woolman. It might mean acts of kindness and integrity in your workplace—enabling the Kingdom to enter your everyday life and transform it.

As you think on these things, remember that you are not alone. Ask God for help. Ask other Christians for their wisdom. Listen deeply. Jesus modeled service for us, and we are called to follow. Go where he leads.

Lord Jesus, you gave us an example of Kingdom enactment. May your kingdom come into my life. Amen.

2. CALLED TO CARE

Then God said, "Let us make humanity in our image to resemble us so that they may take charge of the fish of the sea, the birds of the sky, the livestock, all the earth, and all the crawling things on earth."

Genesis 1:26 CEB

When I was in middle school, I was issued a locker where I kept my textbooks and other possessions. It was a place to stash my lunch at the beginning of the day, and I could decorate it as I saw fit. If I had a girlfriend (it only happened twice during this period), I could tape her photo inside the door, next to a mirror or picture of a sports car. For the year, this space was mine. My locker was subject to my care.

In the Book of Genesis, we see God creating humankind in the divine image, male and female. Human beings are then given a job: to care for the earth and all its creatures. Just as my middle school locker was not mine forever, the earth remains God's possession. Men and women are called to give witness to God through responsible stewardship, just as I was expected, by my middle school principal, to be a responsible steward of school property.

According to today's Scripture, if we serve God faithfully, our lives will "resemble" God. Our care—of our locker or our family, farm, or business—will take on a God-shape. Our care falls under God's care. Knowing, loving, and serving God are cooperative ventures, a grand collaboration enabling us to bring glory to God through our lives.

We are called to care for God's creation. As Dallas Willard writes, "We are, all of us, never-ceasing spiritual beings with a unique eternal calling to count for good in God's great universe."[20] God has given us people, things, and places to care for. God, in turn, calls us to live under his care, being good stewards and living rich lives.

Ask God how your care might be transformed by his, how your calling might be reconceived in light of his commission. Then seek to give witness to the world's true caregiver.

God, you have called me to care, as you care for me. Help me to give witness to your goodness. Amen.

3. GREATER THAN CIRCUMSTANCES

And now, do not be distressed and do not be angry with yourselves for selling me here, because it was to save lives that God sent me ahead of you.

Genesis 45:5

Modern Western culture has great difficulty making sense of suffering. When national tragedies happen, the first question is always, Why? Answers do not come quickly. People turn to religion for a little while. Christianity provides one possible answer, but the answer is filled with tension; it does not fully alleviate our suffering. Instead, Christianity teaches that God works redemptively through suffering. This is not easy to accept.

Today's Scripture tells us Joseph's thinking on the subject. He believed that God journeys with us through the crucible of suffering in order to bring about some greater good—perhaps even a good we are not able to perceive in our lifetimes. Serving God may mean that we must enter and embrace suffering in order for it to be used for purposes greater than our own.

For Joseph, the reasons for his sufferings were made plain to him. If you read the whole of his story in Genesis, you will find a cocky, arrogant kid who, after receiving prophetic visions through dreams, gloated over his siblings and even his parents.

His siblings, jealous and spiteful, sold him as a slave but staged his death, deceiving their father concerning his fate. Later, Joseph served a stint in prison after being framed by his master's wife. But Joseph did not become bitter. Interpreting dreams for high officials in the pharaoh's court, he ascended to the highest position in Egypt, second only to the pharaoh. He was certain God had been at work.

Joseph's story teaches hard lessons. If you are passing through a difficult time, don't lose hope. If you've been in the pit for years, remember Joseph. God is greater than our circumstances. If you truly are hurting, voice your anguish to God; laments are found in the Psalms. But also think of Jesus, who endured the cross. Through his death, Christ secured our forgiveness of sin and union with him. Trust him.

If you want to serve God, know that hard times may come. In those seasons, fix your eyes on Jesus.

God, you are greater than my sufferings and are master over all. If hard times come, increase my faith so that I might serve you well. Amen.

4. EVERYTHING IS BACKWARD

"But many who are first will be last, and the last first."

Mark 10:31

When I lead mission trips, I often observe people who have not learned how to serve. They might be able to put eggs on a plate or clean a few tables, but their attitudes expose them. With a look, they communicate superiority. In conversations processing our experiences, they voice condescension. There is no feeling of generosity or mercy.

As a leader, one of my responsibilities is to teach a new perspective on service and how we relate to our fellow human beings. As a leader, sometimes I'm the one who must learn these things anew. For help, I turn to Mark 10:13-52, from which today's Scripture is taken.

Here Jesus teaches his followers that they must be transformed. The disciples know Jesus is a king, but what kind of king? They are mystified. He places children before them and tells the disciples they must become like kids if they are to enter the kingdom. He speaks of his death, and it doesn't sound royal. His disciples jockey for position, ask questions about who is the greatest, and strive to prove themselves deserving of the best seats in the kingdom. But Jesus keeps defying their categories, saying stuff like the "first will be last, and the last first." He tells them they won't rule like the Gentile kings but will act as servants, and he will lead the way. He'll give his life "as a ransom for many" (Mark 10:45).

We're often like the disciples. We think that once we're tight with Jesus, we're going to have the best seats at the table and all will go well. We think our own self-assurance is enough—why would Jesus have chosen us if we weren't special? But in Jesus' kingdom we're called to serve, not to demand that everyone serve us. We are sent to the world's deep hurts to bring hope. We're called to be like children, to be teachable and to trust in God, not in our own abilities.

We're called to be like Jesus, and, by the power of the Holy Spirit, God will transform us and make us like him. We have much to learn.

Lord, help me to serve as you served, to love as you loved. May I serve the least of these as though I were giving service to you. In Jesus' name. Amen.

5. THE TWIZZLER

If anyone has material possessions and sees a brother or sister in need but has no pity on them, how can the love of God be in that person? Dear children, let us not love with words or speech but with actions and in truth.

1 John 3:17-18

On a long road trip, my friend Steven wanted to illustrate a concept. He pulled out a Twizzler, a flexible stick candy. Without saying a word, he gave the Twizzler to one of the two teenagers in the backseat. Without missing a beat, this young woman tore the Twizzler in half, sharing with her neighbor. Everyone smiled.

In today's Scripture, we are taught about love. Love is revealed in actions, not simply through words. There must be a match between the message and the methods. We see this in Jesus.

In the passage just before today's Scripture we read, "This is how we know what love is: Jesus Christ laid down his life for us. And we ought to lay down our lives for our brothers and sisters" (1 John 3:16). We know Christ's love because of what he did on the cross. We are invited to live a life like his, expressing love through the giving of ourselves.

On our road trip, on a very modest level, this principle was on display. One person received the Twizzler. Instead of hoarding it for herself, she gave to someone who had none. Being a recipient of a gift, she gave. When God gives us love, we must in turn give. All of us are in need of love, and the greatest love is God's, shown to us in the life, death, and resurrection of Jesus. When we serve others, we must remember Christ. We serve in love because we have been claimed by love.

How do we serve? In a way that points back to the love we have received in Jesus. One simple way, described in 1 John, is to give of our material possessions when we see another who has need. In this way, others see the love of God in us and are likewise invited to share in this same love, rooted in Jesus, who laid down his life for us.

Father, warm my heart, set me aflame with your love. May I serve others in a way that gives witness to your son, Jesus. Amen.

Serving with Time

6. HOW WE SPEND OUR LIVES

A person can do nothing better than to eat and drink and find satisfaction in their own toil. This too, I see, is from the hand of God.

Ecclesiastes 2:24

When I wake up each morning, I generally take a look at my daily planner. Each week, I look at the overall flow, Sunday to Saturday, and note the big events on the horizon for that month. And each year, I establish goals and build in time to evaluate my progress. As I assess my schedule, I try to be a good steward of my time.

Each day, we are given the gift of time. The question is not if we will pass the time, but how. In the Book of Ecclesiastes, the writer observes there is "nothing better" than good food, drink, and satisfying work. But do we always see such things as "from the hand of God"? And how does the Christian faith help us steward our days?

Annie Dillard wrote, "How we spend our days is, of course, how we spend our lives. What we do with this hour, and that one, is what we are doing. A schedule defends from chaos and whim. It is a net for catching days. It is a scaffolding on which a worker can stand and labor with both hands at sections of time."[21]

Serving God requires good stewardship of time, whether our moments are spent working, raising a family, or engaging in service opportunities. Rather than thinking narrowly—measuring service to God as time spent in "church activities"—think broadly. Every moment is an opportunity for you to manifest the grace of God, right in the midst of your ordinary, everyday routine.

Of course, this does not mean you should neglect opportunities to serve in mission or engage with "the least of these." Such opportunities are vital for growth in the Christian spiritual life. But as the writer of Ecclesiastes observed, life is made up of so much more. Slow down. Be intentional. Develop a rule, an approach to life that will enable you to derive joy and deep gladness in the moment, recognizing that every breath is a gift of God.

God Almighty, you have ordered the sun and stars, and your love has set the planets in motion. Our days pass according to your word. May I receive each moment as a blessing and steward my time well. Amen.

7. LIFE ON PURPOSE

Teach us to number our days
so we can have a wise heart.

Psalm 90:12 CEB

When my wife and I welcomed our first child to the world, a thoughtful friend gave us a small bundle of twelve placards, one for each month of our daughter's first year. These were to be used in photographs, put on display somewhere within the image. The reverse side of each placard had a few questions to be answered by either my wife or me, noting the changes we had witnessed in our child's life.

We used these placards to mark the time, to create memories of what we witnessed and how our daughter passed her days. We extended this practice to her first day of preschool and to other family moments, and I've made an effort to sit down and write a letter when she does something profound or when I have a hope for her future. I file those notes away for a future birthday.

Most parents would admit that having a child makes the passage of time more perceptible; the changes are always before you. It is only too clear that children do not remain children forever. Concerning our own lives, we are not always so quick to acknowledge our growing older and to number our days. Many of us live in denial about time.

But our mortality is evident and absolute. We will not live forever. We will not remain young forever. And we will not reach the fullness of our human potential until we acknowledge the finitude of our days.

The psalmist's prayer is instructive: "Teach us to number our days so we can have a wise heart." When we accept that our days in a physical body are numbered, we gain perspective, which allows us to measure how each day can be spent well.

When my daughter asks me to dance, I stop what I'm doing and jump in. One day, she may no longer ask. Each day, I assess whether I've spent my moments well—in work or as a parent, a husband, a friend. Sometimes I succeed; sometimes I fail. I learn through both experiences.

How are you spending your days?

Place your life before God. Set a new goal. Dream a new dream. Use your moments for God's glory.

Holy Spirit, search my heart and reveal your wisdom to me. Teach me how to number my days and to live wisely. Amen.

8. A CAUTIONARY TALE

Then he told them a parable: "A certain rich man's land produced a bountiful crop. He said to himself, What will I do? I have no place to store my harvest! Then he thought, Here's what I'll do. I'll tear down my barns and build bigger ones. That's where I'll store all my grain and goods. I'll say to myself, You have stored up plenty of goods, enough for several years. Take it easy! Eat, drink, and enjoy yourself. But God said to him, 'Fool, tonight you will die. Now who will get the things you have prepared for yourself?' This is the way it will be for those who hoard things for themselves and aren't rich toward God."

Luke 12:16-21 CEB

In the early 1990s, users of an Internet forum began handing out tongue-in-cheek honors called the Darwin Awards to people who died "in an extraordinarily idiotic manner."[22] Darwin Award winners have wrongly handled explosives, have swum in swamps teeming with alligators, and have stepped out of speeding automobiles. The stories, often unbelievable, caution us against acts of stupidity and foolishness.

Cautionary tales are helpful in ways different from inspirational stories. Sometimes we need a shock to the system, causing us to reassess where our lives are headed if we're not careful. After reflection, we can correct our course.

Thankfully, the Bible teaches us with examples to avoid and saints to follow. In Luke, Jesus gives us a case study of folly. He is speaking to a crowd of people, and someone shouts, "Teacher, tell my brother to divide the inheritance with me" (Luke 12:13). Jesus answers that he is not the one to settle the matter, then tells the story in today's Scripture.

Jesus might have assumed that his questioner's motivation was greed or sloth. These temptations can lead to a poor use of time. Once the rich man secured an abundance, he intended to hoard it for himself, relax, and enjoy his spoils. But judgment came.

Use your resources, including your time, wisely. You don't know what tomorrow might bring. God has good purposes for you to pursue, blessings to pass on to others. Be rich toward God. Be generous. Be wise, not foolish.

Lord Jesus, may I always live with purpose, using my time and resources in ways that are a blessing to you. In your name. Amen.

9. THE COUNTERCURRENT OF REST

Remember the Sabbath day and treat it as holy.

Exodus 20:8 CEB

The sabbath is such a strange idea: one day in every seven to be kept holy before God? There is so much to do; surely taking one day off is asking too much.

It would be easy to quote statistics on how busy all of us are, but I don't need to reinforce what you already know. Constant motion and stress are likely your standard mode of operation. "Busy" is worn as a badge of honor. In my social circle, it is common for people to answer the question "How are you doing?" with "Busy" rather than "Well."

We are addicted to hurry, busyness, and activity. We believe that our worth and dignity are found in what we do. When asked to reserve one day in seven for a break in activity, for rest and play and worship, we worry that we might lose touch with who we are or lose status in the eyes of our peers and coworkers. But sabbath is the way of wisdom.

For Christians, there is no firm law or command as to when sabbath should be observed. The Book of Hebrews says Jesus is the fulfillment of the sabbath—in him, we have entered an ultimate rest (Hebrews 4:9-10). Besides rest, sabbath can lead to renewal.

155

Routine periods of disengagement or cessation from activity can make space for the mind to create and the body to heal. Slowing down allows us simply to *be* before God and our loved ones, fully present and alive.

Using that one day for worship in community can further Christian growth. Sunday has become a day of worship for Christians, observed in remembrance of Jesus' resurrection. For some people, another day of the week might be better suited.

If you do not worship with a community of Christians, is it because you are too busy? How might adopting a weekly rhythm of worship enable you to connect with God and grow spiritually? Are there commitments or priorities that need to be examined or eliminated to remove hurry and busyness from your life?

Consider your life. Ensure that you are creating margin, room for sabbath rest.

God, help me to practice sabbath, resting before you so that I might be recharged for your purposes. Amen.

10. WANT TO GET AWAY?

Early in the morning, well before sunrise, Jesus rose and went to a deserted place where he could be alone in prayer.

Mark 1:35 CEB

In a course on the Christian spiritual life, one of the requirements was to spend a day in solitude. Our instructor told us to identify a day on the calendar, clear all appointments, and purposefully listen to God, praying and gaining awareness of self. He gave us a few ideas: rent a hotel room, reserve a cabin or campsite, visit a monastery, ask a friend or relative to lend you a spare room. This idea was new to me.

I elected to spend my day at a state park, and I reserved a small cabin. Disengaging from my everyday relationships, turning off my cell phone and not accessing the Internet, separating myself from the sounds of the city—all of it was disorienting at first. But over time I became thankful for release from distractions and focused on prayer. I asked God for vision. I meditated on past events, identifying faults and expressing gratitude for strengths. Solitude allowed me to be present before God in a way I had not experienced.

In the Gospels, we learn that Jesus practiced solitude. He deliberately separated himself from the crowds, his friends, and the demands of his ministry so he could be alone in prayer. We would be wise to follow his example.

If you are an introverted person, you might find it easy to spend time alone but hard to shut down your phone or refrain from other distraction—in my quiet moments, I find it hard not to pick up a book and read. If you enjoy the company of others and constantly seek companionship, then being alone for a time may sound frightening, boring, or a waste of time. Whatever your personality type, you'll discover what Christians throughout time have learned: solitude is an indispensable discipline for growth in the spiritual life.

Plan time for solitude, whether it be a few moments each day, a complete day free from commitment, or three or four days alone in the presence of God. Set aside distractions, follow Jesus' example, and focus on God.

Almighty God, I am constantly distracted. May I place myself alone in your presence, that I might hear your voice, clearly discern your leading, and follow your direction. Amen.

Generosity

11. WHERE IS YOUR HEART?

"For where your treasure is, there your heart will be also."
Matthew 6:21

My first car was a 1987 Chevrolet S-10 Blazer. It had a Blaupunkt tape deck, vinyl interior, and rubber floors. I came to love that SUV. But from the moment my dad gave me the keys, I was looking to upgrade: tinted windows, speakers, a subwoofer and amplifier, a CD player with a detachable face for security purposes. I wanted to pair the simplicity of the vehicle with sound-system sophistication.

It would take money and time.

A friend and I had operated a lawn business for a couple of summers, so I was able to save some money. Once I had a few hundred dollars, I went to Mitch's Car Audio and set up an installation. The result was bliss. For a couple of years of my life, all I thought about was sound. My car sound system was my treasure. My heart was there.

There is an old preacher's maxim that if you want to know your priorities, look at your calendar and checkbook. They will tell you all you need to know.

Where do you spend your time?

How do you use your finances?

Where is your heart?

We can see in today's Scripture that Jesus knew our hearts are reflected in our outward actions. By noting how we spend our money and use our time, we can discern our motivations and something of our character.

But Jesus also knew that an outward view is not enough. The journey to become a deeply committed Christian requires a change of motivation and of the heart. God wants us to give joyfully of our time, money, and other gifts. True generosity, then, reaches beyond our finances but does not exclude them. True generosity is all-encompassing; it is generosity of life.

Do you want such a life? Ask God for guidance. Open your heart to Jesus, seeking an honest assessment of how you utilize your time and spend your money. Ask if the Holy Spirit can show you a better way.

Jesus, you know the human heart. Will you help me discern mine? Lead me. Transform me. Make me a generous person, in every facet of life. Amen.

12. THE KINGDOM ECONOMY

"Sell your possessions and give to the poor. Provide purses for yourselves that will not wear out, a treasure in heaven that will never fail, where no thief comes near and no moth destroys."

Luke 12:33

In the cartoon television series *SpongeBob SquarePants*, Captain Eugene Harold "Armor Abs" Krabs is the owner of the Krusty Krab restaurant. Mr. Krabs is featured in nearly every episode, and a prominent aspect of his character is greed. He pries pennies from the floor, scraps for every extra dollar, employs SpongeBob as a fry cook at a very cheap rate, and always angles for new business.

Mr. Krabs's greed makes him an antagonist in many of the stories; his desire to maximize profit puts extreme demands on SpongeBob, the hero. Mr. Krabs is always anxious concerning the stability of his business. He is a kind of anti-type to SpongeBob, who is happy and carefree. Mr. Krabs constantly accumulates, while SpongeBob most often gives of himself. Through good storytelling, the creators of *SpongeBob* are imparting lessons concerning whom to emulate, and it's not Mr. Krabs.

Jesus preceded *SpongeBob SquarePants* by a few centuries. In his day, as in ours, there were people who sought to amass wealth, hoard their possessions, and build up their storehouses. Abundance of possessions made the people anxious: they worried about thievery, and new things started to seem old. Jesus saw that the things we own can come to possess us.

In today's Scripture, Jesus provided a remedy. Sell your possessions. Give to the poor. Store up your treasure in a place where it won't seem old and can't be stolen. Rather than holding your possessions with a closed fist, open your hand. Give. Be generous. Which story are you living? Are you tightfisted and anxious, possessed by your possessions? Or are the things you own merely gifts to reinvest in the Kingdom, gaining for yourself an eternal possession of joy and thanksgiving to God for his grace?

Today, see and appreciate the abundance God has already given you. Pledge to participate in the divine economy.

Father in heaven, you have given me all I need and more. May I give of myself and find your joy. Amen.

13. THE BAD NEWS AND THE GOOD

People will be lovers of themselves, lovers of money, boastful, proud, abusive, disobedient to their parents, ungrateful, unholy.

2 Timothy 3:2

I have high expectations of other people, especially Christians. I expect people who claim Jesus as Lord to live up to their best ideals. I expect them always to be loving and kind, generous with money, free from greed, abstaining from sin of all kinds, faithful in their marriages, and respectful of everyone. I expect Christians to rise above messiness and tragedy and disappointments.

Here's some bad news: people don't always live up to ideals.

Did you notice anything about the list in today's Scripture? Those were problems in the first century, and they still are problems today. One of the great ongoing realities of human history is that very few of our big problems are ever fully eradicated. Progress is elusive; sin remains. The members of each new generation require transformation; character is always in need of reshaping. We need redemption and renewal, or we'll fall prey to destructive patterns and vice.

Here's some good news: there is hope.

Jesus calls us to be a new people: the church. As the church, we are to be formed in Jesus' way, so that through our relationship with him we will become a radical alternative to the world. Though some people will continue to be vain and greedy, arrogant and brash, we are called to be modest and generous, humble and meek. Christ has led the way. He has provided the means for our transformation and growth, by grace, in holiness. Turn and trust.

We must face another truth that we might be tempted to avoid: often we are the ones guilty of the vices listed in our reading today. Rather than using this text as a club against people outside our community, let's apply it to ourselves. How are we doing? Are we being the people Jesus has called us to be?

I'm a Christian. I don't always live up to the ideals. But Jesus came for the sick, not the healthy, and I need his healing.

Don't we all?

God, you have the power to heal. Take my broken, sinful heart and make it whole, so that I might do the good things you would have me do. Amen.

14. GREAT POWER, GREAT RESPONSIBILITY

Great gifts mean great responsibilities; greater gifts, greater responsibilities!

Luke 12:48*b* *The Message*

One of my favorite comic book heroes is Spider-Man. Peter Parker, an ordinary, bookish teenager, is bitten by a radioactive arachnid and as a result is granted incredible powers. Spider-Man has superhuman agility and strength, can cling to most surfaces, and possesses a sixth sense that alerts him to approaching danger. His drive, ingenuity, and brilliance allow him to engineer web-slinging devices so he can scale buildings and swing high above the city streets. His story is filled with twists and turns as he learns to use his powers for good.

In 1962, the first Spider-Man story concluded with a panel containing this line: "With great power there must also come—great responsibility." The line was spoken in later stories and by Peter Parker's uncle Ben in the 2002 movie, but Jesus stated the principle two thousand years earlier.

Superhero stories captivate us because we know this principle is true. When ordinary people are granted special powers, we want to see how they react. Will they use their powers well? Will they choose the good, or will they go the way of evil? We put ourselves in their place and wonder what we would do. Would we be brave, risking our necks for loved ones, for the city, for the world?

Superhero stories also captivate us because, in some small way, these stories are like our own. We have power and responsibility, however great or small. Whether a person works in building maintenance or is president of the United States, those responsibilities can be carried out poorly or effectively.

God has given us power and responsibility in our communities, our families, our jobs, and our lives. Faithful excellence in each sphere will look different, and we'll need to rely on God to show us how best to serve. Ask God for help. You will receive an answer.

The greater your responsibilities, the greater your potential to do good.

Lord God, I acknowledge that I have been given the gift of responsibility in certain areas of life. May I act for the good of your kingdom. Amen.

15. BECOMING GENEROUS

The generous will themselves be blessed,
for they share their food with the poor.

Proverbs 22:9

In summer 2012, I traveled with a group of teenagers to Minneapolis, Minnesota, where we woke very early the first morning there and arrived at Simpson United Methodist Church. This church, located in a diverse neighborhood, is open for ministry to the poor and homeless in the community. Volunteer groups bring supplies and prepare meals in the church kitchen to provide sustenance for their clients. We had a wonderful experience and were received hospitably by the staff and patrons. Our students, mostly from affluent suburban families, were blessed in sharing with the poor.

Throughout the Bible we read a clear message: those who have much are called to share with those who have little. God wants us to be compassionate toward those who are poor. To do so means acting on a radical understanding of grace and being willing to risk something of our ourselves.

We see these qualities on display in Jesus. Jesus came to offer radical grace and made that grace available through the giving of himself in life and death. Paul wrote, "For you know the grace of our Lord Jesus Christ, that though he was rich, yet for your sake he became poor, so that you through his poverty might become rich" (2 Corinthians 8:9).

We are called to perform acts of mercy as a response to God, who has first been generous to us. By sharing our resources, we express a deeper spiritual reality. Our generosity is a witness to God's grace.

When I followed up with the students about our experience at Simpson, each of them remarked that the gratitude we received was a blessing. The experience of being charitable built our character. It formed us in Christ, so that our future acts of generosity would be given with the gospel in view.

That, after all, is the goal. God desires not only that we perform generous actions, but also that we ourselves *become generous people*, as described in today's Scripture.

Commit to sharing your resources with the poor. As you do so, remember Jesus.

Spirit of God, you have poured out your grace upon us beyond measure. May we be generous as you are generous. In Jesus' name. Amen.

Spiritual Gifts

16. GIFTS FOR GLORY

Each of you should use whatever gift you have received to serve others, as faithful stewards of God's grace in its various forms.

1 Peter 4:10

In the 1985 film *Chariots of Fire*, sprinter Eric Liddell is chosen to run in the Olympics representing Great Britain. The honor, however, comes with a price. Liddell has been called to serve as a missionary to China and must delay his service until the Olympics are concluded.

In one of the film's pivotal scenes, Liddell has an intense conversation with his sister. She pleads with him to leave behind his training and the spectacle of competition and go with her to China.

Her words suggest that she believes Liddell's desire to run is a trifle, ultimately meaningless and unworthy of his time.

But Liddell answers her with conviction: "God . . . made me fast, and when I run, I feel his pleasure." Liddell sees his speed as a gift. By running, he honors his Creator. Whenever he uses his gift, he feels God's affirmation, love, and delight.

All of us have been given a gift, or gifts, that can be used for God's service. Some of us are athletic, while others are academically gifted. Some have business acumen, while others have artistic skill. These gifts are dispensed according to God's grace. Each of us has different gifts, and whatever gifts we have should be used for the glory of God.

What are your gifts? What skills make you unique? How might you use your gifts to serve others, for the good of all?

Sit down with a journal or a trusted friend. Name your talents and skills. Ask if there might be a gift you haven't noticed, something the other person sees that you have not yet perceived. Spend time crafting a vision for how to use your gifts in God's service, perhaps in ways that are new. How can you steward your gifts over the remainder of your lifetime?

God has made you unlike any other person; the gifts you have to offer the world are unique. Use them well.

God, you are the source of every gift. Help me discern my talents and abilities and use them to the fullness of my potential. As I employ the gifts you have given me, may I bless you and bless others. Amen.

17. THE ASSURANCE OF HELP

*"When the Companion comes, whom I will send from the Father—
the Spirit of Truth who proceeds from the Father—he will testify
about me. You will testify too, because you have been with me
from the beginning."*

John 15:26-27 CEB

When I was in elementary school we hosted a classroom presentation of "Jack and the Beanstalk." While donning my costume, I tried to put on a pair of jeans without removing my sneakers. My foot got caught. I was stuck. I needed help.

Thankfully, my teacher, Mrs. Smith, rushed down the hall after being alerted to the trouble. She was gritty and dependable. After she offered a word of assurance and a tug on my foot, I was free. Collecting myself, I delivered my line: "Fee-fi-fo-fum, I smell the blood of an Englishman."

In John 15, the disciples are the ones who are troubled and stuck and worried they will not be able to do what Jesus has called them to do. Jesus, aware of the trouble, assures them of help. He makes a promise, which we read in today's Scripture. The disciples, familiar with the stories of the Old Testament, have heard of times when God's Spirit had come to accomplish a certain task through designated individuals. But Jesus is speaking of something broader, more permanent, and more personal. He states that the Spirit of Truth will rest on the disciples and give them strength and confidence to do everything he had told them to do.

The same promise applies to all who follow Jesus today. When you place your faith in Jesus, you are given the gift of the Holy Spirit, the Companion, the Spirit of Truth, the one sent from the Father. You can rely on the Spirit to help as you witness to others about Jesus. You're not alone. There is help—the assistance of the heavenly kingdom—right there at hand.

Paul writes, "The Spirit you received does not make you slaves, so that you live in fear again; rather, the Spirit you received brought about your adoption to sonship. And by him we cry, '*Abba*, Father.' The Spirit himself testifies with our spirit that we are God's children" (Romans 8:15-16).

What an incredible teaching.

Live by the Spirit.

Holy Spirit, assure me of your presence. Help me to place my trust in you. Amen.

18. BODYBUILDING

Brothers and sisters, I don't want you to be ignorant about spiritual gifts.

1 Corinthians 12:1 CEB

In the 2008 film *City of Ember*, the heroes Lina and Doon must unlock a mystery. The city of Ember is underground, in a cavern so large that full-scale buildings mark the landscape. A generator provides power, but a crisis is looming, as the lights have begun to flicker, which threatens to plunge the city into darkness. The inhabitants have lost touch with history, and though they are aware that their community has existed for nearly 250 years, they do not know how their people came to be there or why. Lina and Doon are certain that something is amiss.

Lina and Doon soon discover a family heirloom containing cryptic documents that they believe will help them solve the mystery. They are convinced that the builders of the city left the papers behind. If they can discern the papers' meaning, perhaps they can discover a way to save Ember. The documents eventually lead them to learn that Ember was intended as a refuge whose preservation systems were made to last 200 years. For some time, the inhabitants have been kept ignorant by corrupt leadership. Lina and Doon discover that liberation is possible, and they take action to save their people.

In today's Scripture, Paul declares that he does not want his fellow Christians to be ignorant concerning spiritual gifts. He would like all Christians to understand the variety and power of their gifts. Unlike the leadership in the city of Ember, Paul urges the people of Corinth to discover the possibilities for their lives. This knowledge could lead to liberation and radical growth.

In the verses that follow, we read about the various gifts given to the Christian community. Paul names wisdom, knowledge, faith, and others. Open your Bible. Read the list. Paul states, "There are different kinds of gifts, but the same Spirit distributes them. There are different kinds of service, but the same Lord. There are different kinds of working, but in all of them and in everyone it is the same God at work" (1 Corinthians 12:4-6).

What is your gift? How are you using it to build up the body of Christ?

Lord, help me to know the gift or gifts you have given me, by your Spirit. May I use those gifts to build up your body. In Jesus' name. Amen.

19. THE POWER FOR MISSION

While they were eating together, he ordered them not to leave Jerusalem but to wait for what the Father had promised. He said, "This is what you heard from me: John baptized with water, but in only a few days you will be baptized with the Holy Spirit."

As a result, those who had gathered together asked Jesus, "Lord, are you going to restore the kingdom to Israel now?"

Jesus replied, "It isn't for you to know the times or seasons that the Father has set by his own authority. Rather, you will receive power when the Holy Spirit has come upon you, and you will be my witnesses in Jerusalem, in all Judea and Samaria, and to the end of the earth."

Acts 1:4-8 CEB

Growing up, my favorite restaurant was a Chinese place called Liang's. Every now and again, my parents would ask our family what we would like for dinner, which meant they were considering take-out; I always voted for Liang's. When I turned sixteen, I became the family's delivery driver. My dad provided a credit card and told me to call in the order. I opened the phone book, dialed the number (which I had underlined), and was off.

Liang's was my mission. The phone book, the phone, my car, and the credit card were my tools. My dad had provided everything

I needed. The work was mine to do, but I couldn't do it apart from what he had given.

In the Book of Acts, the disciples faced a similar situation, though of course for much higher stakes. They had been given a mission. Jesus provided the vision; the Father had given the tools. The disciples were to be witnesses—first in Jerusalem, then in the surrounding region of Judea and Samaria, and finally to the ends of the earth. The Holy Spirit would come upon them and give them power.

The Book of Acts unfolds, the Holy Spirit moves the disciples to live according to Jesus' vision. What began as a small group expands to a worldwide movement. The same power that fueled those first disciples is available to us today, to be received by faith. Trust Christ. Welcome the Holy Spirit. You have a mission. You've been given the tools and the power. Now go and do.

Father, you have promised to give me your Holy Spirit, through faith in Jesus Christ. May I receive the power to do as you have commanded. Amen.

20. TOGETHER EVERYONE ACHIEVES MORE

We have many parts in one body, but the parts don't all have the same function. In the same way, though there are many of us, we are one body in Christ, and individually we belong to each other. We have different gifts that are consistent with God's grace that has been given to us. If your gift is prophecy, you should prophesy in proportion to your faith.

Romans 12:4-6 CEB

Football is one of my favorite sports. On each side of the ball, eleven people work together, serving different functions. Linemen use their girth to open holes for a running back or protect the quarterback from the rush of a defensive player. The quarterback orchestrates his unit at the line of scrimmage, calling signals, changing plays, and handing off the ball or attempting a forward pass. The running backs, receivers, and tight ends are expected to make big-time plays.

Not every body type is suited for every position. Small, speedy players are best equipped to play running back or receiver. Heavyset guys are often best at blocking. But when each player finds an ideal position and does his job well, the team clicks and they can achieve great things.

Whether you enjoy football or basketball, softball or synchronized swimming, the principles of team sports can also apply to the church. We are called to work together. We are incredibly diverse. Not everyone has the same gifts. We need one another to be our best. We need to discern carefully who can do what and to equip each person to use the gifts. As described in Romans 12, prophecy is one of the church's gifts, and Paul wants each person with that gift to use it well "in proportion to your faith." Serving, teaching, encouraging, giving, leading, and showing mercy are other gifts that Paul names.

Every person you encounter in your church has a different set of gifts. We need everyone to participate, for in Christ, "individually we belong to each other." To the degree we work together, God is glorified and the church is strengthened.

Have you found your place in the body of Christ? If so, use your gifts. If not, talk to a pastor or other leader and ask him or her to help you identify ways you're uniquely equipped to bless others.

God, help me to discern my gifts, and to use them well as part of the body of Christ. Amen.

Evangelism

21. THE SOURCE OF GROWTH

Because of this, neither the one who plants nor the one who waters is anything, but the only one who is anything is God who makes it grow.

1 Corinthians 3:7 CEB

I grew up in a church that placed a strong emphasis on evangelism. I'm thankful for this. We were constantly encouraged to share our faith with other people. Most often, this sharing was to take the form of a conversation. My friend Jason was skilled at engaging people in public places—at a pizza place or in a waiting room—and soon he would have the person talking about faith. Jason would then share the good news of Jesus, ask if he could pray, invite the person to our church, and walk away with a story about leading someone to Christ.

That's never been my style. I'm more likely to plant a thought about faith in the mind of a friend or help a committed Christian take the next step. For a while I felt guilty that I wasn't more like Jason. But I see now that that was a mistake—that the work I do is worthwhile and important in God's kingdom.

There are different ways to serve God's kingdom. Some of us are matchmakers, helping people meet God for the first time. Others are foundation builders, giving new believers the information and practices that will serve them for years to come. Still others help raise the building, guiding people to mature and grow and become all that God intends them to be.

Whatever the role, it is God who is at work. When Jason shared his faith and saw people come to believe in Jesus, it was God who brought that to pass. When I have given faithful witness and people have grown in faith, God gets the glory. Whether planting or watering, God is the catalyst for growth.

How do you share your faith? Where do you see God giving you an opportunity to help others know Jesus, either more fully or for the first time?

Be faithful in your calling, sharing the gospel with others as God gives you gifts and opportunity.

God, you are the one who grants the growth. May I see you at work as I seek to share you with others. Amen.

22. PURPOSED FOR ETERNITY

He has made everything beautiful in its time. He has also set eternity in the human heart; yet no one can fathom what God has done from beginning to end.

Ecclesiastes 3:11

What happens to us when we die?

The religions of the world give different answers to this question, and it is worthwhile to consider each view. Investigating these things reveals that the writer of Ecclesiastes was correct: God has "set eternity in the human heart." Eternity is grander than we can fathom, yet our existence forces us to consider it. Where have we come from? Where are we going? And does it matter?

To illustrate eternity, one of my friends took a rope and stretched it full-length across a very large room. Marking a segment with two pieces of blue electrical tape, he asked the rest of us to imagine the rope reaching infinitely in either direction, and to consider the portion between the two pieces of tape as our lives. Knowing that our time is short, how will we live?

The question is a good one, and the implications are staggering. If life is fleeting and time will march on after I am gone, what hope is there to have an impact in the present? Why should I live one way rather than another?

In order for our lives to have meaning and purpose and hope, we need a deeper truth, and Christianity offers it. Life is not meaningless, for God made this world for a purpose. In the Book of Genesis, God speaks the world into existence as a magnificent display of love and creativity. Men and women are designated as stewards of the created order, charged with oversight and care for the creatures and land.

Later, when things go awry, God unveils a plan for redemption, calling a people to enter a covenant relationship with him and working toward restoration of the world. God assures his people that the bad things they experience will turn out for good, the good things they accomplish will never pass away, and the best things are yet to come. In Christ, there is hope for the present and for eternity.

Very likely, your friends and neighbors have quietly pondered eternity. What hope might you offer them, based on Christian faith? Consider the hope you have, and share as you are led.

Eternal God, may I live according to your purposes. You are my hope. Amen.

23. FULLNESS OF LIFE

"The thief comes only to steal and kill and destroy; I have come that they may have life, and have it to the full."

John 10:10

If you could live life to the fullest, what would that entail?

Bungee jumping and cliff diving? Exploring a rainforest or a deep-sea trench? Would you hang glide or parachute? What, exactly, is fullness of life?

Whatever it might be, we want it. We want life to be exciting, full, and worthwhile. We believe our lives are made to count; rightly so. But how? How are we to live in pursuit of the good? What would life entail if, at the end of our days, we could be assured of deep satisfaction and rest? If that kind of life is possible, how do I obtain it?

These are some of the greatest and most perplexing questions ever posed. Philosophers, intellectuals, and everyday people like you and me have debated them. They remain today and are examined on reality television and on the covers of gossip magazines. They echo down the hallways of our universities and governing institutions. Not surprisingly, these questions were asked in the time of Jesus.

The answer Jesus offered is as straightforward as it is enigmatic: Jesus offered himself. "For God so loved the world," we read in the Book of John, "that he gave his one and only Son, that whoever believes in him will not perish but have eternal life" (John 3:16). In the following chapters, Jesus states that "whoever drinks the water I give them will never thirst. Indeed, the water I give them will become in them a spring of water welling up to eternal life" and "I am the way and the truth and the life" (John 4:14; 14:6).

When we tell people about Jesus, we offer them fullness of life, an eternal life, with implications for both present and future. Jesus offers us forgiveness from sin but also teaches and empowers us to show compassion, mercy, and love to a broken and hurting world.

We invite others to believe in Jesus, not only through our message but in our lives.

How are you showing the fullness of life that Jesus offers?

Lord Jesus, you have offered me fullness of life. May I come to understand what that means. May I be a revelation, that others may see it in me. Amen.

24. THE LORD OPENS THE HEART

One of those listening was a woman from the city of Thyatira named Lydia, a dealer in purple cloth. She was a worshiper of God. The Lord opened her heart to respond to Paul's message.

Acts 16:14

Throughout history we find stories of conversion to the Christian faith. In the summer of 386, Augustine of Hippo had one such experience. After Jesus and the Apostle Paul, Augustine was perhaps the most influential figure in Christian history. His life and writings changed the world.

Augustine came to know Jesus after a prolonged intellectual and emotional struggle with the Christian message. In his autobiographical work *Confessions*, Augustine tells of his conversion moment. While walking in a garden, he heard a voice singing, "Take up and read; Take up and read." Opening a nearby manuscript containing the Book of Romans, he read a verse that penetrated his heart. Augustine reflected, "Instantly at the end of this sentence, by a light as it were of serenity infused into my heart, all the darkness of doubt vanished away."[23]

As we read Augustine's story, there is no doubt that God was at work. The same was true in Lydia's case, described in today's Scripture, and in every conversion to Christ.

Often when we share our faith, we place undue pressure on ourselves to bring about a response. We think that if someone is to profess faith in Jesus, we are the key. We need to use the right words and communicate clearly. We need to dismantle all objections so that faith appears reasonable. We act as though conversion depends completely on us, that it is always instantaneous, and that if someone fails to believe, we are to blame.

In evangelism, our responsibility is faithful witness. We present the gospel in word and deed and invite others to join us on the journey. We notice where God is at work in our midst, do our best to understand and explain Christian belief, and live with integrity. We create room for the Spirit of God to work on our hearts and the hearts of our friends. When we see change and movement, we give glory and thanksgiving to God.

Lord, we are called to trust that you are always at work, even when we might not see. Help us to remember that you are the one who draws all people to yourself. Amen.

25. THE MESSAGE
OF RECONCILIATION

So from now on we regard no one from a worldly point of view.
Though we once regarded Christ in this way, we do so no longer.
Therefore, if anyone is in Christ, the new creation has come:
The old has gone, the new is here! All this is from God, who
reconciled us to himself through Christ and gave us the ministry
of reconciliation: that God was reconciling the world to himself
in Christ, not counting people's sins against them. And he has
committed to us the message of reconciliation. We are therefore
Christ's ambassadors, as though God were making his appeal
through us. We implore you on Christ's behalf: Be reconciled to
God. God made him who had no sin to be sin for us, so that in him
we might become the righteousness of God.

2 Corinthians 5:16-21

Growing up, I played with a neighbor boy every day. For reasons I can't recall, one day I decided I no longer wanted to be friends. I crafted a letter expressing dislike for my neighbor. Among other remarks, I wrote, "I hate you." I found a pushpin and posted the note on my neighbor's front door. I might have been in second or third grade at the time. It was not my finest moment.

It didn't take long for my note to be discovered. I did not understand that my actions might destroy the friendship. The next time

I asked the boy's mom if he could play, I got a cold stare and a refusal. A couple of days later, my friend's mom spoke with my parents and arranged a conversation with me about my actions. I felt terrible. Together, we named the wrong and discussed the hurt. I was asked to apologize, and I received forgiveness. That day, there was reconciliation.

When we share the good news about Jesus, we undertake a reconciling ministry. Today's Scripture describes how, once we have been reconciled to God, we become "ambassadors" of God's reconciliation. We want those who have experienced a breakdown in their relationship with God to discover the peace that is possible through the cross and resurrection of Jesus. We want others to experience "new creation."

Spread the message.

Gracious God, you have repaired our broken relationships. Now, you send me forth to share with others the good news that reconciliation is possible. May I do so faithfully. Amen.

Session Six
Serving God Through Social Service

26. IN NEED OF A NUDGE

Jesus said to them again, "Peace be with you. As the Father sent me, so I am sending you." Then he breathed on them and said, "Receive the Holy Spirit."

John 20:21-22 CEB

Outside my bedroom window each year, a robin builds a nest. She lays eggs and keeps them warm, until one day a few small chicks emerge. Before long we see the robin returning to the nest with worms to feed her young, who stretch their necks and open their mouths to receive their food. Our family observes these chicks as they develop and grow strong. Then, when the time is right, the robin nudges her chicks from the nest and they fly away. The chicks were not born to stay in the nest. They were meant to soar.

Sometimes Christians are like those chicks. We hear the message about Jesus, enter his world, and delight in our early growth. We receive teaching from the Bible and attend church meetings. Our needs are met, and we are comfortable. But we were never meant to remain in the nest; God has work for us to do in the world. We need a good nudge to get us going.

In John, Jesus rejoins his followers after the resurrection. They are disoriented and unsure of what will come next. They haven't put together all the pieces of Jesus' message. Jesus reminds them that they have a mission. Just as he was sent from the Father, Jesus sends his followers into the world. In a scene that reminds us of the way God breathed life into the first man in Genesis 2, Jesus breathes on his disciples and tells them to receive the Holy Spirit, who will assist them in the work.

We too have been sent, into our homes and schools and offices to do the work God has given us to do. That might entail being a loving mom or dad, a diligent teacher, or a courtroom attorney committed to justice. Each of us works in a different arena to fulfill our mission. Our calling is to faithfulness, wherever we have been sent.

Jesus did not call you to stay in the nest. You were called to be sent out into the world, working for God's purposes.

God, nudge me from the nest. Put me to work. Amen.

27. AS ONE WHO SERVES

For who is greater, the one who is at the table or the one who serves? Is it not the one who is at the table? But I am among you as one who serves.

Luke 22:27

On a trip to Cedar Rapids, Iowa, one of my teenage friends surprised me. After each meal, when his friends moved on to play or rest, he would stick around and help clear dishes, wash tables, and mop the floor. All the students were invited to do this, but he was the only one who consistently responded.

It quickly became apparent, however, that he hadn't done much of this kind of work. He needed to be trained, so a few of us showed him step by step how to mix cleaning solutions, wipe down surfaces, and use a mop and bucket. My friend was being taught to serve.

We often think of Jesus as an incredible teacher, and Christians confess him as Lord. He was, and is. But in his life, Jesus put himself in the lowest place. He didn't just talk about it; he was a servant of all. Jesus knew that those seated at the table were considered greater than the servants, and he chose to serve.

The way of Jesus is the way we are called to follow. It is the way my teenage friend chose. He wanted to learn how to be truly great by becoming the servant of all. It meant doing jobs that were not honored but were still important. Jesus calls us to do servant-work, to remain humble, and to look out for the interests of others, considering their needs greater than our own. The result is a good and beautiful life, a life more like that of Jesus.

Service to others must be learned, especially if it is to be done with purity of heart and authentic love for the other. How are you learning to serve? Where are you among others "as one who serves," following the way of Christ?

Today, look for an opportunity to serve another person. Give away a coat, hold a door, pick up trash, wash dishes, and do it all with a smile. Follow the way of Christ.

God, may I become the servant of all. Amen.

28. GRACE FOR THE PRISONER

*Continue to remember those in prison as if you were together with
them in prison, and those who are mistreated as if you yourselves
were suffering.*

Hebrews 13:3

Have you ever visited someone in prison? Have you ever been
incarcerated? Columnist Lisa Bloom writes, "We imprison more
of our own people than any other country on earth, including
China which has four times our population, or in human history."[24]
Christians have a calling to those in prison. We are called to care
for those behind bars and to work for a more just society.

My friend Nathan spent many years visiting prisoners, teaching
a Bible study called the Alpha course. Through his experiences
with prisoners, he matured in his faith and found his life transformed. He discovered that those in prison needed to be assured
that they had not been forgotten by those on the outside.

The prisoners had experienced a deep sense of guilt and were
in need of restoration and forgiveness. Some of the prisoners
Nathan befriended had never considered matters of faith, and
he found genuine openness to the gospel. Visiting prisoners also
forced Nathan to confront some difficult things about himself.
Before engaging in prison ministry, Nathan condemned felons and

considered himself morally superior. His experiences with prisoners exposed his sin, called him to repentance, and deepened his understanding of grace.

In Hebrews, the writer encourages Christians to remember those in prison as if they themselves were in chains and to suffer with those who suffer. Believers have taken these words to heart ever since. Through Nathan's story, we can see ways that ministry to those in prison can be a blessing. We can also see how God teaches us new things when we follow the teachings of Scripture.

If you want to get involved, organizations such as Prison Fellowship engage in evangelism and discipleship with prisoners, help those reentering society, and coordinate Christmas gifts for the children of prisoners. Churches in your area may have other opportunities, or you may find that you are called to conduct research and begin an initiative on your own.[25]

Remember those in prison. Extend the love of Christ to them.

Lord, may I be an agent of your grace to those in prison. Amen.

29. MEET THE NEW BOSS.
NOT LIKE THE OLD BOSS.

Whatever you do, work at it with all your heart, as working for the Lord, not for human masters, since you know that you will receive an inheritance from the Lord as a reward. It is the Lord Christ you are serving.

Colossians 3:23-24

I have worked a lot of menial jobs. I've been a yardman, stock boy, warehouse worker, barista, bus driver, even a minister. For the past few years I've been a writer and speaker. The work has never been glamorous. But grass needs cutting, product needs to be shipped and displayed, students need transport, people need the gospel. And if the world was deprived of coffee for one day, what would happen?

Timothy Keller rightly states, "There may be no better way to love your neighbor, whether you are writing parking tickets, software, or books, than to simply do your work. But only skillful, competent work will do."[26] Have you ever considered your work this way?

There are many ways to serve God. The simplest is to take whatever you already do and, as you do it, try to keep in mind that you are serving the Lord Christ. This reframes your day, doesn't it?

What would it mean for you to be a Christian banker, a Christian teacher, or a Christian attorney? How would your work take on a greater sense of dignity and meaning? Every job, no matter how simple, helps humans to flourish. When our work is done with excellence, even if no one else notices, God sees and takes pleasure. We find assurance that our work is not in vain.

Serving God does not require traveling to a radical new setting or forming relationships with an entirely new set of people. But once we have come to believe the gospel, our normal, everyday life is utterly transformed. Every interaction is pregnant with the possibility of grace. Every conversation offers an opportunity to encourage and love and build up. Every small act of service is noted by an Almighty God. The greatness of God is found in his ability to work in and through our daily circumstances. Nothing is beyond or below his concern.

Serve God through your work. Render it an offering to God. Be a blessing.

Jesus, may my every action be conducted as an act of service to you. Amen.

30. GOOD DEEDS ABOUNDING

"You are the salt of the earth. But if the salt loses its saltiness, how can it be made salty again? It is no longer good for anything, except to be thrown out and trampled underfoot.

"You are the light of the world. A town built on a hill cannot be hidden. Neither do people light a lamp and put it under a bowl. Instead they put it on its stand, and it gives light to everyone in the house. In the same way, let your light shine before others, that they may see your good deeds and glorify your Father in heaven."

Matthew 5:13-16

For a time, I worked for a small-town church that wanted to bless its neighbors. The leaders looked for ways to get involved in the community and the world. Some church leaders assembled care packages for soldiers serving in Iraq and Afghanistan. Others gathered birthday party supplies—cake mix, streamers, hats, and noisemakers—for children of families with financial limitations. Some of our older ladies gathered to knit and gave away their creations as expressions of kindness and love. When the church acquired a building, we offered a room for Alcoholics Anonymous meetings. Good deeds abounded.

In today's Scripture, Jesus describes an alternative community and invites his hearers to live in a way that makes them distinct. Jesus' people are to be salt and light. As salt, they act as a preservative and a taste enhancer, stemming decay and drawing out flavors. As light, they are beacons and blessings, drawing attention and illuminating darkness. Jesus says that when we let our light shine, others see our good deeds and glorify God.

How can your church be a light to the world? What part might you play?

Be a blessing. This week, sit down with a few friends. Ask, "What are the deep needs in our community? Are we meeting those needs? If so, can we do it better? If not, how can we get started?"

Start small, but act with great love. You might begin with a neighborhood cleanup or a meal program for college students on a tight budget.

Be creative. Ask God to show you the way.

Father, I wish to bring you glory. May I bless my neighbors, living as salt and light, working for the good of my community. Amen.

Notes

Knowing God

1. Quoted in Andrew S. Finstuen, *Original Sin and Everyday Protestants: The Theology of Reinhold Niebuhr, Billy Graham, and Paul Tillich in an Age of Anxiety* (Chapel Hill: University of North Carolina Press, 2009), 69.

2. C. S. Lewis, *Mere Christianity* (San Francisco: HarperSanFrancisco, 2001), 52.

3. Lewis, *Mere Christianity*, 134.

4. Dallas Willard, *Hearing God: Developing a Conversational Relationship with God*, rev. and exp. ed. (Downers Grove, Ill.: InterVarsity, 2012), 212.

5. Abraham Lincoln, "Second Inaugural Address." http://www.bartleby.com/124/pres32.html (accessed February 25, 2013).

6. Quotations from The Hippocratic Oath, Law Enforcement Oath of Honor, and the Presidential Oath of Office. All can be accessed online.

7. Augustine. *Confessions*. 1.1.1.

Loving God

8. Stephanie Watson, "20 Memorable Epitaphs," accessed March 11, 2013, http://people.howstuffworks.com/11-memorable-epitaphs.htm#page=0.

9. Stanley Hauerwas, *Cross-Shattered Christ: Meditations on the Seven Last Words* (Grand Rapids, Mich.: Brazos Press, 2004), 61.

10. Scott McClellan, *Tell Me a Story: Finding God (and Ourselves) through Narrative* (Chicago: Moody Publishers, 2013), 42.

11. Craig Giammona, "Alabama Police Chief Apologizes to Freedom Rider Congressman," *NBC News Online*, March 3, 2013, accessed March 17, 2013, http://usnews.nbcnews.com/_news/2013/03/03/17167907-alabama-police-chief-apologizes-to-freedom-rider-congressman?lite.

12. Horatio Spafford, "When Peace, Like a River (It Is Well with My Soul)," in *New Baptist Hymnal* (Philadelphia: The American Baptist Publication Society, 1926), 363. This excerpt is from the first stanza. The following stanzas establish the reasons for Spafford's confidence in God: he had seen the fullness of Christ's redeeming work.

13. Jane Winstead, "Horatio G. Spafford: The Story Behind the Hymn 'It Is Well with My Soul,'" accessed online March 17, 2013, http://voices.yahoo.com/horatio-g-spafford-story-behind-hymn-is-1620793.html?cat=38.

14. Lewis, *Mere Christianity*, 205.

15. N. T. Wright, *For All God's Worth: True Worship and the Calling of the Church* (Grand Rapids, Mich.: Eerdmans, 1997), 13.

16. Stanley Hauerwas, *The Peaceable Kingdom: A Primer in Christian Ethics* (Notre Dame: University of Notre Dame Press, 1983), 108.

17. John Wesley, Sermon 39, "Catholic Spirit," at The Wesley Center Online, accessed March 20, 2013, http://wesley.nnu.edu/john-wesley/the-sermons-of-john-wesley-1872-edition/sermon-39-catholic-spirit/.

18. From Wesley's Preface to the 1739 Hymns and Sacred Poems, accessed March 22, 2013, http://www.divinity.duke.edu/sites/default/files/documents/cswt/04_Hymns_and_Sacred_Poems_(1739).pdf.

19. Mario Ledwith, "Pope Francis Ditches St. Peter's Basilica and Will Hold Holy Thursday Mass in a Youth Prison Where He Will Wash and Kiss 12 Inmates' Feet," *The Daily Mail Online*, accessed March 21, 2013, http://www.dailymail.co.uk/news/article-2297020/Pope-Francis-ditches-St-Peter-s-Basilica-hold-Holy-Thursday-mass-youth-prison-wash-kiss-12-inmates-FEET.html.

Serving God

20. Dallas Willard, *The Divine Conspiracy: Rediscovering Our Hidden Life in God* (San Francisco: HarperSanFrancisco, 1997), 21.

21. Annie Dillard, *The Writing Life* (New York: HarperPerennial, 1989), 32.

22. Learn more at www.darwinawards.com. This site makes light of tragedy, which is not my intent. However, all these stories do serve as cautionary tales.

23. Augustine. *Confessions*. 8.12.2.

24. Lisa Bloom, "When Will the U.S. Stop Mass Incarceration?" accessed 4/8/2013, http://www.cnn.com/2012/07/03/opinion/bloom-prison-spending.

25. For more information, visit http://www.prisonfellowship.org/ or http://gbgm-umc.org/mission_programs/mcr/4.35/um.cfm.

26. Timothy Keller, *Every Good Endeavor: Connecting Your Work to God's Work* (New York: Dutton, 2012), 76.

Ben Simpson is a writer, speaker, and theologian residing in De Soto, Kansas. He enjoys spending time with his two children and his wife, Molly, who is a United Methodist elder. Visit his web site, wwww.benjaminasimpson.com, or connect with him on Twitter: @bsimpson.

Each of the Journey 101 authors is on staff at The United Methodist Church of the Resurrection in Leawood, Kansas, where they developed, wrote, and implemented Journey 101 as the basic discipleship course for their congregation of more than 15,000 members. The program has since spread to many churches beyond their home church and denomination.

Carol Cartmill is Executive Director of Adult Discipleship; **Jeff Kirby** is Minister of Adult Discipleship and Men's Ministry; **Michelle Kirby** is Learning Events Program Director.